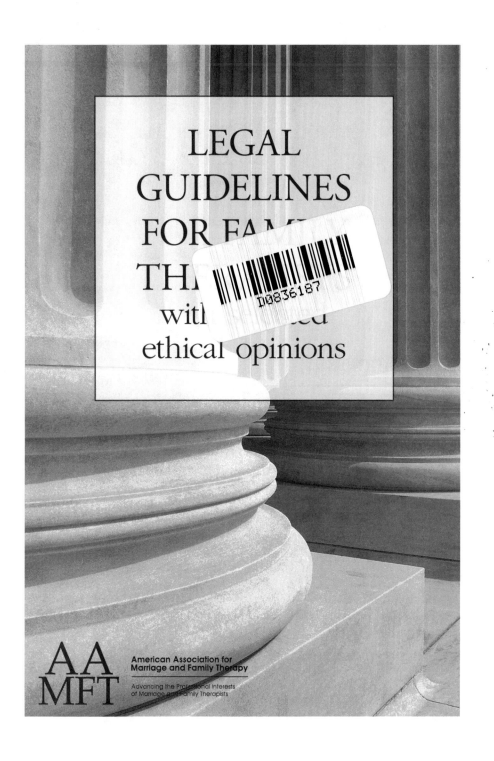

# LEGAL
# GUIDELINES
# FOR FAMILY
# THERAPY
## with related
## ethical opinions

**American Association for
Marriage and Family Therapy**

Advancing the Professional Interests
of Marriage and Family Therapists

# "Legal Guidelines for Family Therapists with Selected Ethical Opinions"

This guide is a collection of information and articles from the AAMFT's Legal and Risk Management Plan. It covers the legal and ethical issues that arise most frequently in practice.

If you face a legal or ethical question in your practice, this guide will assist you.

The contents of the guide are intended for general information only and should not be construed as legal advice or legal opinion. A reader with a specific legal question should consult an attorney since state laws governing the issues addressed here vary considerably.

This guide, or any portion, may not be reproduced without the written consent of the American Association for Marriage and Family Therapy.

© 2007 by the American Association for Marriage and Family Therapy

# Table of Contents

*Section A*

# The Therapist
# and the Office

## Chapter 1
# Getting Started in Private Practice

Once your license is finally issued, you may choose to work in an agency setting (usually a nonprofit and charitable organization or a governmental entity), or you may want to start your own private practice. For many, private practice is a goal they have been seeking from the beginning of their pursuit of the license.

Private practice allows therapists to set their own fees, determine their hours of practice, select the location where they practice, vacation when they want, and decide how small or big their enterprise will be. In essence, private practice allows the licensee to be in charge of his/her own business. It is important for a therapist to consider some legal and business issues when starting or conducting a private practice. This article explores some of the basic issues. Since the laws and regulations of each state vary, it is important to obtain legal or other consultation before action is taken.

## Form of Doing Business/Fictitious Names

The most common form of doing business for marriage and family therapists in private practice is the sole proprietorship. This simply means that you are the sole owner of the business. Thus, the name of the typical practice would be Alice Z. Jones, Licensed Marriage and Family Therapist. Usually, there are no forms to file or documents to execute in order to form a sole proprietorship. Therapists conducting business in this form simply find an office, get business cards and stationery printed, and begin operation. In many jurisdictions (e.g., cities, counties, villages, townships), sole proprietors and others (partnerships, corporations) conducting business in the jurisdiction must first obtain a business license, which is usually only a revenue-raising measure, and requires nothing more than filling out a form and payment of a periodic fee.

If you wish to conduct business under a fictitious business name or trade name, some states require that you obtain permission from the licensing board to use a particular fictitious business name, while other states allow you to use a fictitious name as long as it is not false, misleading or deceptive. In the case of the sole proprietor (an individual), a fictitious business name is generally considered to be a name that does not include the surname of the individual (e.g., Magnolia Street Counseling) or a name that suggests the existence of additional owners (Alice Z.

Jones and Associates). Additionally, some states require that persons using a fictitious business name file a statement with an agency of government, and publish in a newspaper of general circulation a notice which states the true name of the owner of the named business.

States may also require that those doing business under a fictitious business name disclose to the patient, prior to the commencement of treatment, the true name of the licensee (owner) and the fact that he or she is a licensed marriage and family therapist. Such disclosure is appropriate and wise, even if not required by law or regulation. For example, when MFTs and others practice in what might be termed a "loose group" (advertising to the public as the XYZ Counseling Center while each of the therapists is actually conducting a sole proprietorship), it is important that the patient understand who is ultimately responsible (legally and ethically) for the care being provided. In other words, who owns the business where treatment is being rendered? (See Subprinciple 8.3 of the AAMFT Code of Ethics.)

Another form of doing business is the partnership, where two or more practitioners co-own the business and split profits and losses, usually pursuant to a written partnership agreement. The independence of the sole proprietorship is lost when doing business as a partnership, because each partner will have some right to determine how all aspects of the business are conducted. From a liability standpoint, since partners generally act as agents of the partnership, each partner is liable for the negligent acts of the other partners. It is usually unlawful for a marriage and family therapist to be in a partnership with a physician or a psychologist, since the only people who can lawfully receive money for medical services or psychological services are physicians or psychologists, respectively. Thus, most partnerships are between professionals holding the same license.

Many states have passed laws that allow for the formation of professional corporations. The most important caveat with respect to the professional corporation (which can usually be formed by one or more licensees) is that, unlike a regular general business corporation, formed primarily to limit the liability of the individual owners (shareholders), the professional corporation usually does not limit the liability of the health care practitioner for his/her own professional negligence. Legislatures have deemed such a limitation of liability as being against public policy. Similarly, limited liability companies may not be a lawful option for health care practitioners in many states.

Some states allow for interdisciplinary professional corporations. For example, a physician is allowed to be a shareholder or employee of an MFT corporation and an MFT can be an owner (shareholder) or employee in a medical corporation under California law. The significance of this, from a business standpoint, is that an MFT Professional Corporation can lawfully deliver and bill for medical services rendered by a physician. (Remember, each state has its own laws and regulations, so legal consultation is required.) State law may require the name of the corporation to contain certain words or language and may require that the corporation register with the Board (State). It is important to determine whether state law allows for the professional corporation to do business under a fictitious name, and whether or not other requirements (e.g., filings, disclosures) exist.

Generally, unless a private practitioner has been advised that there are tax advantages (e.g., the ability to shelter more income) to incorporation, or unless there is a desire to co-own an interdisciplinary practice, incorporation may not be a compelling option. While professional incorporation may limit some kinds of liability (for example, if the patient slips and falls on a defective rug in the therapist's office), it appears that such limited benefit is not by itself sufficient to convince most therapists to incorporate. Malpractice and related insurance coverage provides therapists with protection in case they are held liable for professional negligence or for negligently maintaining their premises.

## Fee Setting

One of the disclosures that must be made to a patient, prior to the commencement of therapy, is the fee to be charged for the services that are to be rendered. Many therapists make this disclosure as part of a more general disclosure statement required by state law or dictated by sound and ethical professional practice. Therapists are generally free to set their own fees in accordance with what they think is appropriate for the clientele they expect to see and the services to be rendered. The importance of being clear when it comes to the issue of fees cannot be over emphasized. The AAMFT Code of Ethics, in Principle VII, provides excellent guidance to private practitioners and others with respect to the issue of fees and other financial matters.

Some therapists choose to make clear to patients that if they are unable to continue to pay the agreed-upon fee, the therapist may terminate therapy (before a large arrearage accumulates) and refer the patient to a low-cost counseling center or an appropriate governmental agency. It is, of course, possible that the therapist may choose to lower the fee (or charge nothing) and continue to see the patient. If the patient is suicidal or otherwise seriously impaired, ethics and prudence may dictate that treatment should continue, at least for some period of time. Otherwise, the therapist may be dealing with an allegation of abandonment.

If a therapist decides to raise his/her fees at a given point in the development of his/her practice, there are two ways that is usually done. One is to raise the fee only for new patients. Some believe that raising fees during the course of therapy is exploitive because the patient is not in a good bargaining position when confronted with the request for additional money from the therapist. The AAMFT Code of Ethics provides that patients are to be given reasonable notice of any changes in fees or other charges. Fees should probably not be raised during the course of therapy unless the patient has been informed, in advance of commencing treatment, of the possibility that fees and charges may increase. It is helpful if the therapist also lets the patient know that fees will not increase more than once a year, and that the amount of the increase will not exceed a specified percentage.

Many therapists want to adopt a "sliding fee scale." Depending on the nature of the practice, a sliding fee scale is often impractical and awkward for private practitioners. It is more likely to be used in nonprofit and charitable corporations, where the fee to be charged can be determined by the income level of the patient and the family. Private practitioners in most professions generally charge a set fee - their usual and customary fee. They are free to make exceptions and see someone for a lower fee or for no fee.

Setting a "usual and customary fee," with the right to make exceptions, is simple and easy to administer. It lets patients know what you think your time and ability are worth. When dealing with insurers and other payers, it provides consistency to your profile. If fees vary, based upon the economic circumstances of the patient, including the presence or absence of insurance coverage, insurers may take the position that your fees are being artificially and improperly raised when there is insurance coverage. Depending upon the facts and circumstances, this kind of billing practice may constitute insurance fraud.

## Liability/Insurance

Therapists and other practitioners are liable for their negligent or intentional acts or omissions that cause harm to the patient. Generally, in order to avoid liability, a therapist must act as a reasonably prudent practitioner holding the same license would have acted under like or similar circumstances. Generally, honest errors in judgment do not necessarily constitute negligence or result in liability. Employers are usually liable for the negligent acts of their employees. A supervisor is liable for his/her own negligence in providing supervision, but does not automatically become liable for the negligence of the supervisee, unless the supervisor is also the employer. Before deciding to hire professional employees (licensees or interns), consider the advantages and disadvantages of becoming an employer.

Active private practitioners must at all times have insurance coverage for malpractice (professional liability) claims or lawsuits. Therapists should not skimp when it comes to protecting themselves with the maximum coverage they can obtain. It gives therapists peace of mind and prepares them for the worst-case scenario. Most malpractice insurers also provide coverage for legal representation at depositions and at disciplinary proceedings before the licensing board.

Do not allow your policy to lapse for any period of time. A therapist risks a suit for negligence that occurred during any interruption in coverage. They became personally exposed to not only a monetary judgment against them, but also to the rather substantial costs of an adequate legal defense. This can also happen to practitioners who put their licenses on inactive status and cancel their insurance. Shortly after doing so, a former patient contacts the therapist during a crisis and the therapist steps in to help, ever so briefly. In such a situation, the therapist is "bare" (personally exposed) for the negligence that may occur during the period he/she is without professional liability coverage.

## Advertising

Most businesses, including small health care practices, implement an advertising plan or strategy of some proportion. Some may desire to advertise in newspapers, TV, radio and even outdoor advertising (bus stops, billboards), while others may advertise directly to lawyers or physicians. Some may only seek a listing in the Yellow Pages or another directory. Others may advertise over the Internet. Most will advertise by giving out their business cards within the community where they practice and elsewhere. AAMFT's Code of Ethics (Principle VIII) provides guidance for those who choose to advertise in any way or to any degree. From a legal standpoint, most state laws allow health care practitioners to advertise in any way or media, but prohibit advertising that is false, fraudulent, misleading, or deceptive.

States have imposed a variety of other requirements, such as a mandate to use the state license number in any advertisement. Also, those who conduct business under a fictitious business name may be required to make disclosures regarding the actual ownership of the business. With respect to advertising about fees or the costs for services, some laws prohibit the use of certain language (e.g., "lowest fees"). At least one state bars any statement, endorsement, or testimonial that is likely to mislead or deceive because of a failure to disclose material facts.

*Chapter 2*
# Forms For Use In Your Practice

There are many sources for practice forms. Some states require that a client record contain specific forms or specific content. Some states require disclosure forms that provide specific information to clients. An informed consent form can be the basis for your agreement with a client and limit your risk for records requests and court appearances.

You can use an office policies document to state your records retention and destruction policy. You can supplement your informed consent document with additional information where the client is a minor child and the parents are divorced. Some states grant specific rights to non-custodial parents with respect to the records of a minor child. Some states specify the amounts that can be charged for record production at the request of a client. Some states permit minors to seek therapy without parental consent.

An informed consent/consent to treat/disclosure document is strategic documentation: a document that demonstrates that what the practitioner did was appropriate, correct and required.

Even though a court may not interpret your informed consent document as a legally binding contract, it is evidence of the confidentiality of the therapy relationship, and of notice to the client of the limits on your participation outside the treatment context. Some courts give consideration to the document when making a determination about whether to quash a subpoena.

At a minimum your informed consent document should address the following areas:

- Nature, purpose, and anticipated course of services
- Limits of confidentiality
- Explanation of client identity/no secrets policy
- Records requests/client's right of access to records/ privacy policy
- Fees and billing arrangements (including collection practices and charges for court)
- Insurance reimbursement, if applicable
- Emergency procedures for contacting therapist

Remember that state law and regulation may have other or additional requirements for a disclosure or informed consent document.

## Chapter 3
# Keeping Clinical Records — Legal and Ethical Issues

State law and MFT regulation may be more specific with respect to the issues presented here.

## Why Keep Records?

Aside from the fact that it may be required, it is good business practice to keep records of the transactions and occurrences within any business. With respect to health care professions, the need for good record keeping is more important, since the mental or physical health of a patient is involved, as well as significant marital, family, and other interpersonal relationships. Some therapists say that they keep minimal records in order to protect the privacy of the patient. There may be more protection for the therapist and the client from laws governing confidentiality and client privilege, and from HIPAA'S Privacy Rule.

Good record keeping is important both to clients and to therapists. Clients may need to prove their mental status or that they suffered emotional distress or other impairment. The need to do so may arise in a custody or visitation proceeding, in a civil lawsuit for damages, in a workers' compensation or disability case, for a security clearance, or for some other reason. Clients depend upon their therapists to keep adequate and accurate records, which can provide proof that the client is, for example, being treated for a particular mental disorder. Additionally, patients have a right to expect that, if they were to obtain treatment at a later time from another practitioner, the records from the prior therapist would be available to the new therapist, if needed.

Good record keeping can help the therapist establish that he/she acted appropriately if sued by the patient for negligence, or in a disciplinary proceeding by the licensing board or an investigation by an ethics committee. When a patient attempts or commits suicide, for example, or causes physical harm to others, the therapist is sometimes the target of an investigation or lawsuit to determine whether or not the therapist acted appropriately. A member of a couple or family receiving services may try to hold the therapist responsible for a divorce or separation or for the loss of custody or visitation rights. Well-documented records can help the therapist prove that he or she acted reasonably.

## Content of Records

Some state laws or regulations specify the content required to be in records maintained by MFTs and/or other licensed health professionals, while other state laws take a different approach and leave actual content to the discretion of the therapist. California law, for example, states that it is unprofessional conduct if an MFT fails to keep records consistent with sound clinical judgment, the standards of the profession, and the nature of the services being rendered. This kind of statute provides flexibility for the practitioner. Arizona, on the other hand, sets out, 12 separate items to be included in a client record.

HIPAA's Privacy Rule, in creating a right of access to information in the record, lists documents that, if they exist, are available to the client: medication prescription and monitoring, counseling session start and stop times, the modalities and frequencies of treatment furnished, results of clinical tests, and any summary of the following items: diagnosis, functional status, the treatment plan, symptoms, prognosis, and progress to date. AAMFT's Code of Ethics requires that MFTs maintain accurate and adequate clinical and financial records. It is always important to accurately document all billings and payments so as to avoid fee disputes with patients.

Helpful documentation includes any consultation had with other practitioners who have confirmed or expressed support for the therapist's treatment approach. Both the fact of the consultation, and the substance of it, can often help to prove that the therapist was not negligent. Even though professional opinion and judgment may differ, the therapist may have acted competently and appropriately, albeit not perfectly. Another useful thing to document is the fact that the therapist has referred the patient to a physician for a medical exam, or to a psychiatrist for medication, or to other licensed practitioners for testing or other services.

Therapists must often balance competing interests when determining record content. This is especially true in the emerging area of "psychotherapy notes." (See discussion below.) Sometimes a therapist may want to omit or excise a name from the record in order to protect the client or a third party. If a client were having an extra-marital affair, for example, the patient and the therapist might be more comfortable if the name of the paramour was omitted from the record.

## Who Owns the Records?

Some states are very specific that the mental health professional owns the record, while a client has a right to get a copy. Even in those states that do not have a specific law or regulation regarding record ownership, the therapist can argue that the client came for therapy, not for record creation or record keeping.

A client who requests that the therapist destroy all treatment records on termination of the relationship is probably concerned about privacy and confidentiality, or upset about the results or direction of the therapy. While the client can request and receive a copy of most of the contents of the file, the client cannot direct destruction of the record.

Questions related to client access to records are best addressed as part of the informed consent discussion at the beginning of the therapeutic relationship. A Notice of Privacy Practices, required for HIPAA covered entities, or a Notice of Client Rights Under the Privacy Rule might avoid surprising the client when, for example, you require a request for records to be made in writing or paid for in advance.

Record ownership can also be an issue when an employee of an agency or private practice leaves the employment voluntarily or is fired. A rule of thumb is that an employee does not own the client or the client record and is not entitled to "take" clients or their records. If the employee negotiates with the employer so that clients are permitted to leave the agency and follow the therapist, the agency or other entity should keep a copy of the record in case some question arises about the client's treatment while a client of the agency. If the client remains with the agency, the departing therapist has no need for a copy of the record. Indeed, it is grounds for quashing a subpoena for records that the therapist does not have the records requested, and that the subpoena should be directed to the agency or entity.

If the relationship between the therapist and agency or entity is that of principal and independent contractor, it is more likely than not that the independent contractor agreement addresses the issue of client and record ownership.

## Safe Maintenance of Records/Destruction

Therapists have a duty to protect the privacy of client records. Thus, therapists must take care to safeguard records, and to the extent possible, prevent records from being lost, stolen, or viewed by "third parties." This usually translates into keeping records in a locked file cabinet in the therapist's office. The therapist's office also should be locked when it is not being used. Client files should not be left in public areas, where they may be seen or taken. Whether records are kept on a computer or otherwise, the records should only be available to those who need to have access in order to carry out the therapist's business. Computer screens should be placed and used in a manner that does not allow viewing by others. Computer records should be regularly and promptly backed up so that they are not lost due to technical error or failure.

A common mistake is permitting records to be taken from the premises where they belong (e.g., a private practice, clinic, or nonprofit organization). This is often done in order to accommodate an intern or trainee who is receiving off-site supervision. If the supervision cannot take place onsite, it is important to take certain precautions. For instance, if records are to be taken for the benefit of the supervision, take a copy rather than the original file. Ideally, take only portions of a file, or alter information regarding the client's identity. Interns and trainees who transport records should keep the records under their personal control at all times, and not to leave the records in a car or in someone's office or residence.

When records are destroyed, after passage of the appropriate amount of time (see

Ethical Advisory Opinion on Record Retention and Destruction), they should be destroyed in a manner that preserves confidentiality by shredding or burning. Records should not be placed in a trash bag for disposal by others, nor should records be abandoned or left behind.

## What if the Records Are Lost, Stolen or Destroyed?

If records are lost or stolen, the therapist may want to reconstruct the records for treatment purposes. Of course, the ability to reconstruct will depend upon the complexity of the case and the length of time that the client has been in treatment. Records from former providers can usually be obtained again. The primary fear of the therapist when records are lost or stolen is that confidential information will be seen by someone, thus violating the client's right to privacy and confidentiality. Therapists may face the dilemma of whether or not to tell the client of the loss as soon as discovered, or whether to make some attempt to recover the records before telling the client.

Therapists are often reluctant to tell the client, either because they don't want the client to be alarmed and suffer emotional distress, or because they do not want the client to blame them for improperly handling or protecting the records. There may be times when the client is in such mental or emotional condition as to warrant the therapist keeping the loss of records from the client, at least for some period of time. It is important to make sure that this reason is only used when supported by the clinical evidence, and not as part of an effort to hide the fact that privacy may have been compromised.

The facts of each situation should be evaluated, but consider choosing prompt notification of the client. This may, in some cases, subject the therapist to some liability for the negligent handling or maintenance of the records, but in many cases, the therapist may have done nothing wrong. Perhaps there was a burglary, or a hurricane or other natural disaster. Prompt disclosure to the client reduces the likelihood that the client would question why the therapist kept the loss secret.

Prompt and full disclosure is easy when the therapist has not acted negligently. Suppose, however, that a licensed supervisor or employer allows a trainee or intern to take records from the premises and bring them to an off-site supervisor. What if the intern negligently protected the records and now they are missing? Perhaps the intern left the records in an unlocked car or in a briefcase that was misplaced. And further, perhaps a copy of the records was not made. Is the supervisor or employer going to want to immediately notify the patient of the missing records and the details of their loss? The supervisor or employer faced with such a dilemma will want to consult with legal counsel, who will help to evaluate the situation and to hopefully minimize the harm done to the patient and to the employer or supervisor.

## What if the Therapist Moves or Retires?

Some state laws require a therapist to publish, usually in the local newspaper, the fact of a move from the area or retirement so that former clients who may need their records will know, or be more likely to know, the location of the records. With respect to patients who are in treatment at the time the therapist decides to move or retire, therapists should notify patients as early as possible and should document such action in their records.

In states that have no requirements for notice of a move or of retirement, therapists should consider either publication of a notice in a newspaper, or direct notice by letter to the former clients. If using direct notice by letter, consider whether contacting the former client risks compromising the client's privacy.

In most states, licensees are required to notify their licensing board of any change of business address. Additionally, retired licensees can put their licenses on inactive status. Thus, a state licensing board can usually help a client find a therapist who has moved or retired.

If you are required to notify your licensing board of a change of business address, and if there is no requirement to publish the fact of the move or retirement, notice to former patients may be unnecessary. Of course, if you have retained the records as long as required, they can be destroyed. In that case, the issue of notice to the patient is moot. There is generally no requirement that the patient be notified prior to a lawful destruction of records.

*Chapter 4*
# HIPAA Notice For Covered Entities Sample

Health Insurance Portability and Accountability Act of 1996 (HIPAA) has four parts. If you transmit any health care information in electronic form, you are a covered provider and should have a "Notice of Privacy Practices" to give to clients at the first visit. The client should acknowledge, by signing your informed consent/disclosure document, that the client received a copy of the Notice.

### NOTICE OF PRIVACY PRACTICES
THIS NOTICE DESCRIBES HOW MEDICAL INFORMATION ABOUT YOU MAY BE USED AND DISCLOSED AND HOW YOU CAN GET ACCESS TO THIS INFORMATION. PLEASE REVIEW IT CAREFULLY.

## What is "Medical Information"?
The term "medical information" is synonymous with the terms "personal health information" and "protected health information" for purposes of this Notice. It means, in essence, 1) any individually identifiable health information (either directly or indirectly identifiable), whether oral or recorded in any form or medium, that is created or received by a health care provider (me), health plan, or others and 2) that relates to the past, present, or future physical or mental health or condition of an individual (you); the provision of health care (e.g., mental health) to an individual (you); or the past, present, or future payment for providing health care to an individual (you).

*I am a mental health care provider. More specifically, I am a Marriage and Family Therapist, licensed by the State of _____ (State) through the _____ (licensing authority). I create and maintain treatment records that contain individually identifiable health information about you. These records are generally referred to as "medical records" or "mental health records," and this Notice, among other things, concerns the privacy and confidentiality of those records and the information contained therein.*

## Uses and Disclosures Without Your Authorization — For Treatment, Payment, or Health Care Operations

Federal privacy rules (regulations) allow health care providers (me) who have a direct treatment relationship with the patient (you) to use or disclose the patient's personal health information, without the patient's written authorization, to carry out the health care provider's own treatment, payment, or health care operations. I may also disclose your protected health information for the treatment activities of any health care provider. This too can be done without your written authorization.

*An example of a use or disclosure for treatment purposes:* If I decide to consult with another licensed health care provider about your condition, I would be permitted to use and disclose your personal health information, which is otherwise confidential, in order to assist me in the diagnosis or treatment of your mental health condition.

Disclosures for treatment purposes are not limited to the minimum necessary standard because physicians and other health care providers need access to the full record and/or full and complete information in order to provide quality care. The word "treatment" includes, among other things, the coordination and management of health care among health care providers or by a health care provider with a third party, consultations between health care providers, and referrals of a patient for health care from one health care provider to another.

*An example of a use or disclosure for payment purposes:* If your health plan requests a copy of your health records, or a portion thereof, in order to determine whether or not payment is warranted under the terms of your policy or contract, I am permitted to use and disclose your personal health information.

*An example of a use or disclosure for health care operations purposes:* If your health plan decides to audit my practice in order to review my competence and my performance, or to detect possible fraud or abuse, your mental health records may be used or disclosed for those purposes.

*PLEASE NOTE: I, or someone in my practice acting with my authority, may contact you to provide appointment reminders or information about treatment alternatives or other health-related benefits and services that may be of interest to you. Your prior written authorization is not required for such contact.*

## Other Uses and Disclosures Without Your Authorization:

I may be required or permitted to disclose your personal health information (e.g., your mental health records) without your written authorization. The following circumstances are examples of when such disclosures may or will be made:

1) If disclosure is compelled by a court pursuant to an order of that court.

2) If disclosure is compelled by a board, commission, or administrative agency for purposes of adjudication pursuant to its lawful authority.

3) If disclosure is compelled by a party to a proceeding before a court or administrative agency pursuant to a subpoena, subpoena duces tecum (e.g., a subpoena for mental health records), notice to appear, or any provision authorizing discovery in a proceeding before a court or administrative agency.

4) If disclosure is compelled by a board, commission, or administrative agency pursuant to an investigative subpoena issued pursuant to its lawful authority.

5) If disclosure is compelled by an arbitrator or arbitration panel, when arbitration is lawfully requested by either party, pursuant to a subpoena duces tecum (e.g., a subpoena for mental health records), or any other provision authorizing discovery in a proceeding before an arbitrator or arbitration panel.

6) If disclosure is compelled by a search warrant lawfully issued to a governmental law enforcement agency.

7) If disclosure is compelled by the patient or the patient's representative pursuant to local law or by corresponding federal statutes or regulations (e.g., the federal "Privacy Rule," which requires this Notice).

8) If disclosure is compelled by local law governing abuse, neglect or domestic violence (for example, if I have a reasonable suspicion of child abuse or neglect).

9) If disclosure is compelled or permitted by the fact that you are in such mental or emotional condition as to be dangerous to yourself or to the person or property of others, and if I determine that disclosure is necessary to prevent the threatened danger.

10) If disclosure is compelled or permitted by the fact that you tell me of a serious threat (imminent) of physical violence to be committed by you against a reasonably identifiable victim or victims.

11) If disclosure is compelled or permitted, in the event of your death, to the coroner in order to determine the cause of your death.

12) As indicated above, I am permitted to contact you without your prior authorization to provide appointment reminders or information about alternatives or other health-related benefits and services that may be of interest to you. Be sure to let me know where and by what means (e.g., telephone, letter, e-mail, fax) you may be contacted.

13) If disclosure is required or permitted to a health oversight agency for oversight activities authorized by law, including but limited to, audits, criminal or civil investigations, or licensure or disciplinary actions. The __

_____ (licensing authority), which issues licenses to marriage and family therapists, is an example of a health oversight agency.

14) If disclosure is compelled by the U. S. Secretary of Health and Human Services to investigate or determine my compliance with privacy requirements under the federal regulations (the "Privacy Rule").

15) If disclosure is otherwise specifically required by law.

*PLEASE NOTE:* The above list is not an exhaustive list, but informs you of most circumstances when disclosures without your written authorization may be made. Other uses and disclosures will generally (but not always) be made only with your written authorization, even though federal privacy regulations or state law may allow additional uses or disclosures without your written authorization. Uses or disclosures made with your written authorization will be limited in scope to the information specified in the authorization form, which must identify the information "in a specific and meaningful fashion." You may revoke your written authorization at any time, provided that the revocation is in writing and except to the extent that I have taken action in reliance on your written authorization. Your right to revoke an authorization is also limited if the authorization was obtained as a condition of obtaining insurance coverage for you. If local law protects your confidentiality or privacy more than the federal "Privacy Rule" does, or if local law gives you greater rights than the federal rule does with respect to access to your records, I will abide by local law. In general, uses or disclosures by me of your personal health information (without your authorization) will be limited to the minimum necessary to accomplish the intended purpose of the use or disclosure. Similarly, when I request your personal health information from another health care provider, health plan or health care clearinghouse, I will make an effort to limit the information requested to the minimum necessary to accomplish the intended purpose of the request. As mentioned above, in the section dealing with uses or disclosures for treatment purposes, the "minimum necessary" standard does not apply to disclosures to or requests by a health care provider for treatment purposes because health care providers need complete access to information in order to provide quality care.

## Your Rights Regarding Protected Health Information

1) You have the right to request restrictions on certain uses and disclosures of protected health information about you, such as those necessary to carry out treatment, payment, or health care operations. I am not required to agree to your requested restriction. If I do agree, I will maintain a written record of the agreed-upon restriction.

2) You have the right to receive confidential communications of protected health information from me by alternative means or at alternative locations.

3) You have the right to inspect and copy protected health information about you by making a specific request to do so in writing. This right to inspect and copy is not absolute - in other words, I am permitted to deny access for specified reasons. For instance, **you do not have this right of access with respect to my "psychotherapy notes." The term "psycho-therapy notes" means notes recorded (in any medium) by a health care provider who is a mental health professional documenting or analyzing the contents of conversation during a private counseling session or a group, joint, or family counseling session and that are separated from the rest of the individual's medical (includes mental health) record.** The term excludes medication prescription and monitoring, counseling session start and stop times, the modalities and frequencies of treatment furnished, results of clinical tests, and any summary of the following items: diagnosis, functional status, the treatment plan, symptoms, prognosis, and progress to date.

4) You have the right to amend protected health information in my records by making a request to do so in a writing that provides a reason to support the requested amendment. This right to amend is not absolute - in other words, I am permitted to deny the requested amendment for specified reasons. You also have the right, subject to limitations, to provide me with a written addendum with respect to any item or statement in your records that you believe to be incorrect or incomplete and to have the addendum become a part of your record.

5) You have the right to receive an accounting from me of the disclosures of protected health information made by me in the six years prior to the date on which the accounting is requested. As with other rights, this right is not absolute. In other words, I am permitted to deny the request for specified reasons. For instance, I do not have to account for disclosures made in order to carry out my own treatment, payment or health care operations. I also do not have to account for disclosures of protected health information that are made with your written authorization, since you have a right to receive a copy of any such authorization you might sign.

6) You have the right to obtain a paper copy of this notice from me upon request.

*PLEASE NOTE: In order to avoid confusion or misunderstanding, I ask that if you wish to exercise any of the rights enumerated above, that you put your request in writing and deliver or send the writing to me. If you wish to learn more detailed information about any of the above rights, or their limitations, please let me know. I am willing to discuss any of these matters with you.*

## My Duties

I am required by law to maintain the privacy and confidentiality of your personal health information. This notice is intended to let you know of my legal duties, your rights, and my privacy practices with respect to such information. I am required to abide by the terms of the notice currently in effect. I reserve the right to change the terms of this notice and/or my privacy practices and to make the changes effective for all protected health information that I maintain, even if it was created or received prior to the effective date of the notice revision. If I make a revision to this notice, I will make the notice available at my office upon request on or after the effective date of the revision and I will post the revised notice in a clear and prominent location.

As the Privacy Officer of this practice, I have a duty to develop, implement and adopt clear privacy policies and procedures for my practice and I have done so. I am the individual who is responsible for assuring that these privacy policies and procedures are followed not only by me, but by any employees that work for me or that may work for me in the future. I have trained or will train any employees that may work for me so that they understand my privacy policies and procedures. In general, patient records, and information about patients, are treated as confidential in my practice and are released to no one without the written authorization of the patient, except as indicated in this notice or except as may be otherwise permitted by law. Patient records are kept secured so that they are not readily available to those who do not need them.

Because I am the Contact Person of this practice, you may complain to me and to the Secretary of the U.S. Department of Health and Human Services if you believe your privacy rights may have been violated either by me or by those who are employed by me. You may file a complaint with me by simply providing me with a writing that specifies the manner in which you believe the violation occurred, the approximate date of such occurrence, and any details that you believe will be helpful to me. My telephone number is _____ _____. I will not retaliate against you in any way for filing a complaint with me or with the Secretary. Complaints to the Secretary must be filed in writing. A complaint to the Secretary can be sent to U.S. Department of Health and Human Services, _____. [locate regional address at http://www.hhs. gov/ocr/hipaahealth.txt.]

If you need or desire further information related to this Notice or its contents, or if you have any questions about this Notice or its contents, please feel free to contact me. As the Contact Person for this practice, I will do my best to answer your questions and to provide you with additional information.

*Chapter 5*
# Notice Of Health Care Information Practices Sample

Even if you are not a covered entity under HIPAA because you do not transmit health care information in electronic form, HIPAA's Privacy Rule, as well as most state laws, gives a client a right to "inspect and copy" certain information in the client's mental health record.

It is in your best interest to include a notice of your health care information practices as part of your informed consent/disclosure document and discussion.

Each sample also includes a paragraph about the availability of a minor child's mental health record to a parent.

## NOTICE OF INFORMATION PRACTICES
## (TEXAS)

I keep a record of the health care services I provide. You may ask for a copy of that record. You may also ask to correct that record. I will not disclose your record to others unless you direct me to do so or unless the law authorizes or compels me to do so.

Section 611.008 of the Texas Health and Safety Code gives a patient a right of access to recorded health care information upon written request. That Section does not give you a right to a copy of my "psychotherapy notes," which means notes that I prepare that record or analyze the conversation during a counseling session. If your attorney serves me with a subpoena to produce documents or to testify in any court or agency proceeding as a result of our therapeutic relationship, I will produce only those documents that state and/or federal law require that I produce to you. I will not produce psychotherapy notes to you or to a lawyer.

Under Section 611.008 of the Texas Health and Safety Code, I have 15 days to provide a copy of the recorded health care information after receiving the written request.

Under Section 611.008 of the Texas Health and Safety Code, I am permitted to charge a reasonable fee for providing the health care information, and I am not required to give a patient the copy until the fee is paid unless there is a medical emergency. My fee for providing the health care information is 65 cents per page for the first thirty pages and 50 cents per page for all other pages.

Section 153.073 of the Texas Family Code

gives a parent appointed as conservator full and equal access to medical, dental, psychological, and educational records of a child. If you are requesting recorded health care information with respect to your child(ren) under this section of Texas law, your written request must be accompanied by proof of your status as conservator.

# NOTICE OF INFORMATION PRACTICES
## (Washington State)

I keep a record of the health care services I provide. You may ask for a copy of that record. You may also ask to correct that record. I will not disclose your record to others unless you direct me to do so or unless the law authorizes or compels me to do so.

Section 70.02.080 of the Revised Code of Washington gives a patient a right of access to recorded health care information upon written request.

Under that Section, I have 15 working days to provide a copy of the recorded health care information after receiving the written request.

Under that Section, I am permitted to charge a reasonable fee for providing the health care information, and I am not required to give a patient the copy until the fee is paid. The Health Care Information Access and Disclosure law defines a reasonable fee as 65 cents per page for the first thirty pages and 50 cents per page for all other pages.

Section 26.09.225 of the Revised Code of Washington gives a parent full and equal access to education and health care records of a child. If you are requesting recorded health care information with respect to your child(ren) under this section of Washington law, your written request must be accompanied by proof of your status as parent.

## Chapter 6
# Withholding Records From
# A Client Who Doesn't Pay

A former client is asking for a copy of his/her records. The client stopped coming to therapy and owes me $400. Can I demand payment before I turn over the records?

**Subprinciple 7.3: Marriage and family therapists give reasonable notice to clients with unpaid balances of their intent to seek collection by agency or legal recourse. When such action is taken, therapists will not disclose clinical information.**

**Subprinciple 7.6: Marriage and family therapists may not withhold records under their immediate control that are requested and needed for a client's treatment solely because payment has not been received for past services, except as otherwise provided by law.**

First recourse is "informed consent" or other document that the client signed at the beginning of therapy. If your current document does not speak to payment arrangements, you may want to modify it.

Subprinciple 7.6 alludes to a therapist's ethical duty to continue to act in the clinical best interests of former clients. From a business standpoint, a therapist has the right to pursue payment for services rendered and to use legitimate means for seeking collection when payment is past due.

When a client who owes fees makes a request for clinical records, a therapist may see this as an opportunity to obtain some leverage in the struggle to obtain payment and could be tempted to make fulfillment of the client's request contingent upon payment.

When it is foreseeable that doing so could harm the clinical best interests of a former client because the records are needed for the former client's current care, Subprinciple 7.6 is a bar. When in doubt, it would be wise to err in the direction of providing the clinical records, while continuing to use other legitimate means to resolve the debt.

If you have a client who owes you money, the ethical limitation on your seeking collection is 7.3's "reasonable notice." You can provide this notice by sending a letter with return receipt requested (to show the client received it), making a demand for payment of the outstanding balance, and stating that if you do not hear from the client by a specific date (three to four weeks is usually enough notice), that you will turn the account over for collection or file a suit in small claims court.

## Chapter 5
# Licensing Board Complaint

Forty-eight states and the District of Columbia regulate the practice of marriage and family therapy. One function of a regulatory board is the investigation of complaints against license holders. The State board can receive complaints from many sources including liability insurance companies, professional associations, law enforcement agencies, or regulatory boards in other states or provinces. Any client, family member or concerned citizen can file a complaint with a State licensing alleging that a license holder has violated the licensing law or board regulations.

Each State's board has its own rules and regulations for investigating complaints against license holders. Some investigations involve sending a copy of the complaint and asking you to respond. This means you have to sift through the complaint and try and determine what board rule or regulation may have been violated. Other investigations involve board or staff review of the complaint and a letter outlining the facts of the complaint and how those facts state a violation of the licensing law or regulations.

Although easier said than done, if you receive a complaint from your board, don't panic. The first step is to make sure that you are actually the therapist involved. The complainant or the board could have made a mistake. If you recognize that the complaint is from someone you know or treated, locate the file and refresh your recollection about the case. You may have documents that refute the complaint. For example, a former client claims you breached his confidentiality and you have a signed release in the file. You may want to contact your malpractice insurer to find out whether assistance is available in responding to a licensing board complaint.

A growing number of licensing board complaints involve custody or visitation disputes. A parent who loses custody may blame the therapist for the court's order. You may want to take some steps to reduce your risk including additional material and disclosures in your informed consent document and discussions where the clients are or may become involved in a custody dispute.

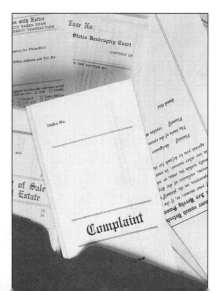

The same informed consent considerations apply to clients who come to you as the result of a court order requiring therapy. Can parties who seek therapy as the result of a court order give informed consent? What is the limit on confidentiality protections for a client unit/participant where the object of the therapy is a report to the court or to Child Services? What protection does the therapist have from a malpractice claim or board complaint by a losing litigant where a therapist's report is part of the court record?

## Chapter 8
# Duty To Report Colleague

D oes the duty to report a colleague's misbehavior trump the colleague's confidentiality rights?

AAMFT's *Code of Ethics* requires you to comply with local law. It does not impose an independent reporting requirement in an instance where a colleague is violating state law. The Code's preamble states "Marriage and family therapists are strongly encouraged to report alleged unethical behavior of colleagues to appropriate professional associations and state regulatory bodies." Certain impaired practice statutes require colleagues to report a practitioner under the influence of drugs or alcohol unless the information came to the colleague in a confidential setting. Another option to consider is approaching the colleague in the spirit of "friendly remonstrance" in keeping with the tradition of self-regulation and maintaining high standards within the profession.

Another alternative to reporting a colleague is to deal with the situation clinically and work towards a self-report. Certainly you want to avoid breaking confidentiality, even if therapy has terminated, given the absence of a clear legal mandate to do so. The AAMFT Code does not mandate reporting, and it would be a violation of the Code to break confidentiality unless the law requires it.

Immunity is often conferred by statutes that require or encourage colleagues to report the unethical behavior or impaired practice of others. In order for that immunity to be effective, however, you need first-hand knowledge of the behavior.

You are encouraged to report unethical behavior of colleagues. However, because you are not mandated to do so, it would not be a violation of the *Code of Ethics* if you did not report your colleague to AAMFT.

Call your licensing board to see if you are mandated to report your colleague to your state or province. At least a few states have laws mandating such reporting, at least in cases of impaired practice.

*Section B*

# The Therapist
# and the Client

## Chapter 1
# Disclosures In the
# Informed Consent Document

*I do a lot of couples therapy. In the last several years, there's been an increase in requests for records/deposition notices by one member of the couple where a divorce proceeding has been started. Can I use my informed consent document to advise clients that I don't testify in legal proceedings?*

Subprinciple 1.2: Marriage and family therapists obtain appropriate informed consent to therapy or related procedures as early as feasible in the therapeutic relationship, and use language that is reasonably understandable to clients. The content of informed consent may vary depending upon the client and treatment plan; however, informed consent generally necessitates that the client: (a) has the capacity to consent; (b) has been adequately informed of significant information concerning treatment processes and procedures . . . (d) has freely and without undue influence expressed consent; and (e) has provided consent that is appropriately documented. . . . .

Subprinciple 2.2: Marriage and family therapists do not disclose client confidences except by written authorization or waiver . . . . When providing couple, family or group treatment, the therapist does not disclose information outside the treatment context without a written authorization from each individual competent to execute a waiver. . . . .

Informed consent is a concept that is generally used to advise a patient of the limitations on confidentiality and fee structure. A typical informed consent document might state the instances where the therapist would have to disclose otherwise

confidential information (child sexual abuse, elder abuse, a threat of violence of a third party, or suicide.) The typical consent form might then discuss the policy regarding payment and whether fees would be charged for canceled sessions and so forth.

As an advice document, the informed consent would be the appropriate time and place to advise couples, families or groups that all therapy participants have to agree to a waiver of confidentiality. It would also be appropriate at that time to discuss the therapist's participation in any litigation that might result in the future and secure the client's agreement.

Whether a client's agreement not to involve

the therapist in future litigation is enforceable is a different issue. The judicial process is separate from and often not controlled by the client. For example, a client may file a lawsuit, and mental or emotional distress may be an element of damages claimed. The defendant in the lawsuit will make demands on the therapist for records and testimony to show that the client's distress is unrelated to the defendant's actions. The client has not involved the therapist and has not breached the agreement.

A therapist can certainly use a non-litigation section in the informed consent document to identify fees and charges for the therapist's time and expenses if a subpoena is issued.

## Chapter 2
# Selected Issues in Confidentiality

The cornerstone principle of the various mental health professions is confidentiality. This legal and ethical principle is critical to successful work with clients, since clients must be assured of confidentiality in order for them to share with their therapists the most private, intimate and sometimes embarrassing details of their lives. The likelihood of clinical success is increased when the client feels comfortable sharing such details with the therapist. Clients put a lot of trust in their therapists, especially with respect to confidentiality. A wrongful breach of confidentiality not only subjects the therapist to civil and administrative liability, but also can have a lasting effect on the client's mental health and how the client views the profession.

## Some General Rules

The first general rule to remember is that you should not release information about a client without the client's signed authorization. Another general rule is that when you release confidential information, only release the minimum amount of information necessary to accomplish the purpose of the release. A third general rule to remember is that when in doubt, resist releasing information and opt in favor of maintaining confidentiality. Ordinarily, there is greater risk in releasing information without the client's authorization then there is in preserving confidentiality. Since these are "general" rules, there are exceptions.

With respect to requiring a client's signed authorization prior to the release of confidential information, there are times when therapists must disclose information without a signed authorization and times when they may do this. Child abuse and elder abuse reporting laws are well-recognized mandatory exceptions to the general rule. Permissive disclosures would typically include cases where a therapist, among other things, has reasonable cause to believe that the client is a danger to self or to others.

Additionally, certain forms of child abuse and elder abuse may not require reports but may permit reports to be made. Under HIPAA (for covered providers) and some state laws, therapists are permitted to make disclosures without the client's written authorization for purposes of the provider's treatment, payment and health care operations.

Releasing the minimum amount of information necessary to accomplish the purpose of the release is a common practice that has been adopted in HIPAA regulations. The therapist confronts this when insurance companies want to see a client's entire file. Therapists should attempt to narrow the insurer's request and to provide only the relevant portion of the records. In situations where a warning has to be (or may be) made to the intended victim of the client's threatened violence, as in the *Tarasoff* case, the warning should generally be concise, direct and limited in scope. The minimum necessary rule is inapplicable in certain circumstances. For instance, it doesn't apply to releases of confidential information by a health care provider for purposes of treatment of the client, where full and complete information is helpful to proper treatment. It doesn't apply to a client's request for a copy of his/her records, and it generally doesn't apply in cases where there is a written authorization.

With respect to the general principle of "when in doubt, resist disclosure," therapists will typically not get in trouble if they resist when in doubt, as long as they make reasonable attempts to ascertain the appropriateness or necessity of disclosure. This principle comes into play with great frequency (and with frequent mistakes by therapists) when an attorney asks the therapist to make and sign a declaration, usually in a divorce/custody proceeding, about one of the parties, or when a client asks the therapist to write a letter to the attorney. While the facts and circumstances vary in these kind of proceedings, the therapist should make sure that the file contains written permission from all of those who might argue that they were entitled to confidentiality.

## The Fact of the Relationship

You should treat the fact of the relationship as confidential. In other words, you should not tell anyone who your clients are or acknowledge that you are treating a particular client. It is not unusual for a therapist to be asked by a law enforcement officer, some other governmental official, or perhaps by a family member, whether or not the therapist is treating a particular client. The answer, given in your own words and style, is "none of your business." If one were not treating the person inquired about, I would not acknowledge that fact, but decline to respond to the inquiry. Simply put, the identity of the client is confidential.

Some may take issue with this principle, since it is not unusual for therapists and counseling agencies to have waiting rooms where clients see other clients and where names are sometimes called out. Clients may also be seen entering the offices of therapists, and in smaller communities, the identity of such clients may be apparent. To arrange office visits otherwise, would probably make people think that there is something wrong with going to a therapist's office and would increase the stigma of mental health treatment even more. Actually, some clients prefer telephone or Internet therapy for the very reason that they seek privacy.

Another thing to consider about the fact of the relationship (as opposed to the content of the therapy) is whether or not you have the client's permission to write to them, call them, or otherwise communicate with them at their home or at some other place. Perhaps the spouse or partner does not know that the client is in therapy, and perhaps the client is not ready to reveal this fact. A letter or bill sent by the therapist may be seen by the spouse or partner and may cause problems for the client, even if it is marked "confidential." Yet another consideration is whether or not the client would want you to acknowledge them should you unexpectedly bump into them in a public place. These issues should be considered, discussed, and clarified with clients early in the relationship.

The fact of the relationship comes into play with respect to pursuing a client or ex-client for monies owed. Some state laws contain provisions that clarify that it is not a violation of confidentiality or of the psychotherapist-patient privilege to sue a client (usually in small claims court) for monies owed. Similarly, therapists and other health practitioners sometimes send unpaid bills to a collection agency. (Use of a collection agency should, if possible, be avoided and only be done with care and with prior notice to the client.) Generally, these actions do not constitute a breach of confidentiality so long as the disclosures made reveal only the fact of the relationship and the amount owed, and not the content or substance of the therapy. If the law were otherwise (each state's law varies to some degree, so therapists must determine what their state law allows), therapists would be unable to collect monies that were lawfully due them.

## Crimes of the Client

State laws usually address the issue of confidentiality and specify the exceptions to confidentiality. It is important to be familiar with the laws in the state where you practice so that violations of confidentiality do not occur. Generally (but not always) the past crimes of a client, revealed to the therapist during therapy, are confidential. Many clients tell therapists about past crimes, such as possession or sale of controlled substances, driving while intoxicated, stealing from an employer, or committing a violent crime. Therapists routinely keep such information confidential. Of course, child abuse and neglect reporting laws and elder or dependent adult abuse reporting laws are well known exceptions to the general rule.

Prospective violence, either communicated to the therapist or assessed by the therapist, presents a different situation. Under these circumstances, disclosure by the therapist may be mandated or permitted, depending upon state law. In short, therapists are usually at least permitted to break confidentiality when the client is in such mental or emotional condition as to be a danger to self or to others, and disclosure is necessary to prevent the threatened danger. Imminent threats of violence against readily identifiable victims, communicated directly to the therapist by the client, trigger (in some states) the so-called "duty to warn."

## AIDS/HIV Disease

Suppose a client tells the therapist that the client has been diagnosed with AIDS. What is the duty of the therapist, if any, to break confidentiality and warn sexual partners of this fact? Or, is the therapist to treat this information as confidential? Generally, and almost universally, this information is confidential, even where the client reveals that he/she is continuing to have sexual relations with one or more partners. This duty of confidentiality arises both as a result of legislation that specifically protects such affected clients from disclosures by health care providers as well as from the general duty of confidentiality. Some have argued that there is or ought to be a "duty to warn," like in the famed *Tarasoff* decision, but others have pointed out that "*Tarasoff* situations" involve serious (and imminent) threats of violence, communicated by clients to therapists, against readily identifiable others.

Some have also argued that while no duty to warn may exist, therapists are permitted to warn because the client is, under circumstances where no disclosure of the condition is made by the client to a sexual partner, a "danger to others." However, the *Tarasoff* "danger to others" standards must usually be as the result of the mental or emotional condition of the client. The danger here is usually the result of a physical disease or condition that may or may not be transmitted, not as the result of a mental or emotional condition. Additionally, the *Tarasoff* "danger to others" is usually the danger of physical violence, such as homicide.

Even if your terminally ill client is in such a mental or emotional condition as to be dangerous — if the client were to tell the therapist that his/her remaining goal is to infect as many people as possible and to take others down with him/her — still, it is arguable that confidentiality should be maintained (unless there is specific statutory instruction to the contrary). If the state wants to impose a duty to warn under these or similar circumstances, the duty (and liability for failure to warn) ought to be imposed on the client, not the therapist whose duty it is to keep communications confidential. Therapists can act by, among other things, discussing the option of full disclose by the client to sexual partners and by discussing other possible changes of client behavior.

# Chapter 3
# Duty To Warn And/Or Protect

You will probably face a situation sometime during your professional careers when you will be treating a client who presents a physical danger to others, to self, or to the property of others. In such situations, the dilemma is whether or not the therapist is required or permitted to break confidentiality in order to protect the client or others from harm.

The duty of confidentiality for mental health practitioners is both an ethical and legal imperative. State laws require confidentiality and provide for disciplinary action, including revocation of license, for violations of the duty. Breaching confidentiality also subjects a practitioner to liability for damages in malpractice suits. The codes of ethics for all mental health professions address the issue of confidentiality, and membership in a professional association can be terminated or otherwise limited for violations of the duty. The duty of confidentiality is not absolute. Therapists are well aware, for example, of their duties to report suspected child abuse and elder or dependent adult abuse.

The famous *Tarasoff v. Regents of the University of California* decision created a new duty for California therapists in 1976. Many other states follow this California decision, and some states have enacted laws that codify the so-called "*Tarasoff* duty." State laws may so therapists should know what the "duty" is in the states where they practice.

The key language from *Tarasoff* states that "[w]hen a therapist determines, or pursuant to the standards of his profession should determine, that his client presents a serious danger of violence to another, he incurs an obligation to use reasonable care to protect the intended victim against such danger." "Serious danger of violence" is used rather than "danger of serious violence." In other words, the threat must be imminent

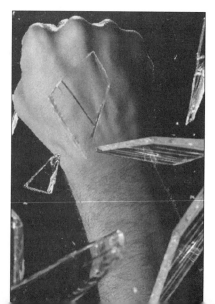

– it is a serious threat rather than a mere "huffing and puffing" in a moment of anger or a conditional threat that may or may not be executed in the future.

It is not uncommon for therapists to ask what their duty is when the client tells them that someone else has communicated to the client a threat of violence against the client or a third party. The *Tarasoff* decision and most state laws are concerned with threatened violence by the client, not by some other party. Unless state law provides otherwise, this situation would require the therapist to keep the communication confidential.

One other portion of the *Tarasoff* decision

is instructive, since it reinforces the importance of confidentiality. The court stated: "We realize that the open and confidential character of psychotherapeutic dialogue encourages the client to express threats of violence, few of which are ever executed. Certainly, a therapist should not be encouraged to routinely reveal such threats; such disclosures could seriously disrupt the client's relationship with his therapist and with the persons threatened. To the contrary, the therapist's obligations to his client require that he not disclose a confidence unless such disclosure is necessary to avert danger to others, and even then that he do so discreetly, and in a fashion that would preserve the privacy of his client to the fullest extent compatible with the prevention of the threatened danger."

# Chapter 4
# Duty To Warn

*I have a client who is HIV-positive and engaged in unprotected sex with his partner. Do I have a duty to warn the partner?*

Subprinciple 2.1: . . . . Therapists review with clients the circumstances where confidential information may be requested and where disclosures of confidential information may be legally required.

Subprinciple 2.2: Marriage and family therapists do not disclose client confidences except by written authorization or waiver, **or where mandated or permitted by law**. . . . .

Subprinciple 3.2: Marriage and family therapists maintain adequate knowledge of and adhere to applicable laws, ethics, and professional standards.

This is a situation where ethical considerations are affected by legal considerations. Everybody has heard of *Tarasoff*, and it is *Tarasoff* that has resulted in that part of your informed consent document where you disclose that everything the client says is confidential except a stated intent to harm others.

Is the risk of HIV infection a circumstance in which confidentiality can be broken because an HIV positive client is placing a third party in clear danger of HIV transmission? Some states have broadened the *Tarasoff* standard by enacting legislation that allows physicians, under certain conditions, to disclose the status of a patient to the spouse of that patient. For mental health professionals, however, there are no legal directives regarding confidentiality and the protection of third parties from HIV infection. The client is not threatening to commit serious and imminent physical violence — the *Tarasoff* standard.

As the therapist, you should, of course, counsel the client about the need for disclosure and the need for preventing exposure. The Centers for Disease Control has program information directed to partner counseling and referral for HIV prevention. One recommended method is to have the therapist be present when the client notifies the partner. Another method recommends that the therapist and client agree on a date and, if the client has not notified the partner by that date, the client agrees that the therapist should notify the partner. The agreement will serve as a waiver of the client's confidentiality rights if the client fails to notify the partner.

## Chapter 5
# Duty To Report

*When I was in the grocery store yesterday, I saw a woman shaking a child in the candy aisle. As a mandated reporter, do I have to report this?*

Subprinciple 2.2: "Marriage and family therapists do not disclose client confidences except by written authorization or waiver, or where mandated or permitted by law. Verbal authorization will not be sufficient except in emergency situations, unless prohibited by law. . . . ."

A duty to report is purely a creature of state law. Mandatory reporters are most familiar in the case of child or elder abuse or neglect. In those cases, the state law requirement would be one of the situations "mandated . . . by law" and would require breach of the client's confidence.

The duty to report should be one of the instances in your "informed consent" document. The client is given notice that, as a mandatory reporter, you are required to breach confidence if the client discloses conduct that you are required by law to report.

State laws identifying those occupations and professions that are mandatory reporters should also set out the requirements of a mandatory report. In most cases, mandatory report laws require that the reporter have acquired the information in the course of practice of the profession. Consequently, seeing the child shaken in the grocery store does not trigger a duty to report. The laws will be specific about the time limits imposed. Some states require mandatory reporters to file abuse or neglect reports within 48 hours of acquiring the information. The laws will also be specific about the agency where the report should be filed. You may not be discharging your obligation to report if the law requires you to notify the police and you call Social Services.

In most states, the child abuse and neglect reporting laws provide mandated reporters with immunity from civil and criminal liability for making reports that are required or authorized. Some states require that the report be made "in good faith," but, in general, there can be no liability for making a required report.

## *Chapter 6*
# Mandated Reporter Questions

Each state has passed some form of mandatory child abuse and neglect reporting act. Some states have imposed similar reporting requirements in the case of elder abuse or neglect. MFTs, as mental health care professionals, are mandated reporters. It is critical that an MFT have detailed knowledge about the child abuse and neglect reporting laws, since a failure to report or failure to report within a specified time is often treated as a crime, and can lead to disciplinary action by the licensing board and liability (money damages) in a civil lawsuit.

Most reporting laws provide **immunity** from civil and criminal liability for making a report. The immunity laws will often protect the therapist, even if the therapist was negligent in concluding that a report was required. Some states require that, in order to be entitled to the immunity, the mandated reporter have acted "in good faith."

In most child abuse and neglect reporting laws, a **child** is defined as a person under the age of 18. One of the important issues involving age is the question of whether there is a requirement to report abuse of a person who is now an adult, but who tells the therapist about abuse occurring in the past when the client was under 18. The abuse could have taken place a few weeks ago or many years earlier. In some states it is reasonably well established that there is no duty to report under such circumstances. In fact, if a report were made, the therapist might not be entitled to immunity, since it was not a report that was either required or authorized by the reporting law.

The **standard for reporting** child abuse or neglect differs somewhat from state to state. Some states use "reasonable cause to believe" as the standard while others use "reasonable suspicion" as the standard. Other statutes require the reporter to "know or suspect." It is helpful, especially when dealing with questionable reporting situations, to know the statutory standard. The basic question is whether you need a mere suspicion, a reasonable suspicion, or something closer to probable cause in order to be mandated to report child abuse.

**"Physical abuse"** of a child is usually considered to be a physical injury inflicted by other than accidental means. Depending upon applicable state law, slapping, spanking or other non-severe forms of corporal punishment that result in no physical injury may not amount to child abuse. Reportable **"sexual abuse"** of a child usually includes sexual assault (e.g., rape, incest, sodomy, or oral copulation) and sexual exploitation (e.g., employment of a

minor to perform obscene acts or assisting a child to engage in prostitution).

**"Neglect"** is generally defined as the neglectful treatment or maltreatment of a child by any person responsible for the child's welfare. It typically includes both acts and omissions. General neglect involves the negligent failure of the responsible person to provide adequate food, shelter, clothing, medical care, or supervision. Severe neglect involves the custodian's intentional failure to provide adequate food, clothing, shelter, medical care or supervision. In most states, neglect must be reported, whether general or severe.

With respect to **"emotional abuse"** or **"mental suffering,"** there is usually no question about reporting severe emotional abuse—it generally will be mandated. Handcuffing a child to the bed or locking the child in a closet (where no physical injury is involved) is an example. Excessive scolding, punishment, blaming and belittlement for insufficient reasons may also be considered to be severe emotional abuse.

The time and manner of reporting varies from state to state. Generally, a **telephone report** must be made immediately or as soon as possible. A **written report** may also be required to be made within a short period of time. Reports are usually required to be made to a designated child protective services agency or a law enforcement office such as the police or sheriff. The reporting duty is generally considered to be an individual duty and cannot be delegated. Some states have enacted laws that prevent employers of mandated reporters from taking sanctions against such employees who may make a report even though the employer has instructed that no report be made.

## Chapter 7
# Treating Children – Selected Legal and Ethical Issues

This article explores some of the common legal and ethical issues that may arise when a therapist agrees to treat a child. It provides some general guidance for navigating through this area of practice. Each state may have its own law applicable to MFTs requiring something other than what is suggested or mentioned in this article. Therapists should always comply with the laws in their states.

## Parental Consent to Treatment

The general rule is that either parent has the right to obtain medical or mental health care for their minor children. Likewise, each parent has a general duty to care for the child, and, where necessary, to obtain needed medical or mental health care for the child. Therapists usually want to obtain the consent of both parents before agreeing to treat a child to avoid problems and disputes and to involve both parents in the treatment, where such involvement is appropriate.

There are, however, many circumstances (e.g., one parent incarcerated or otherwise out of the picture) where a therapist can appropriately and lawfully treat children with the consent of only one parent. Therapists who agree to treat under such circumstances must use good judgment in deciding whether the circumstances justify seeing the child with the consent of only one parent. The therapist must think of both the legal requirements of consent and the clinical considerations, since the absent or non-participating parent may later come forward to object to the treatment, demand that it stop, threaten to sue or complain to the licensing board, or request a copy of the minor's records.

If the therapist is confident that the judgment used was reasonable under the circumstances presented, the solution is often not very difficult. Some therapists who face such situations simply inform the parent that the treatment of the child was consented to by the other parent (and therefore lawful), and that the therapist is not of a mind to abandon the patient by a quick and clinically unwarranted termination. The threatened complaint or lawsuit usually does not materialize. In the event that they do materialize, the therapist will have malpractice insurance

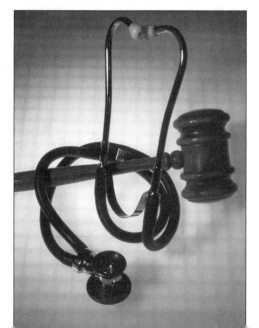

that provides coverage for, among other things, defending a lawsuit and defending a disciplinary matter (complaint to the licensing board).

As to access to the child's records, therapists may be required by state law to permit access even to non-custodial parents under specified circumstances. It is critical for therapists to know this particular state law or regulation in precise detail.

## Determining Custody

In cases where a court has entered a custody or visitation order, ask for a copy of the order to determine the nature of the custody arrangement. In most states, custody has two components: "legal custody" (who has the legal right to make decisions on behalf of the child relating to the child's health, education and welfare), and "physical custody" (with whom the child resides). When a court orders "joint legal custody," this usually means that the parents share the right and responsibility to make important decisions on behalf of their child. In other words, either parent may consent to the treatment of the child, unless the court has specified in the order that the consent of both parents is required.

Suppose the court order confirms that the parents share joint legal custody, and the therapist, with the consent of one parent, commences treatment of the child. Later, the other parent comes forward and demands, among other things, that the therapist stop treating the child. You can suggest to the objecting parent that he or she talk with his/her attorney to confirm the authority of the parent who sought treatment for the child.

The therapist may be uncomfortable interpreting the terms of the court order or determining whether or not the conditions in the court order have been satisfied. For instance, the court order might order joint legal custody but specify that the parties "consult" with one another prior to obtaining "medical care" for the child. What if one parent says that they have "consulted" with the other parent and that such other parent does not want the child to be in psychotherapy? Does "medical care" include counseling by an MFT? If in doubt, the therapist can decline to treat or request the consent of both parents.

## Exercising Discretion

Suppose a parent seeks treatment for a child, and the therapist determines that the parent has been awarded visitation (but no physical custody) and joint legal custody (without a requirement for the consent of both). The parent seeking treatment for the child requests that the other parent not be informed of the treatment of the child. While the therapist may be permitted by law to treat the child with the consent of the parent who has joint legal custody, sound discretion may indicate otherwise. Suppose, however, that treatment of the child does begin. What might the therapist experience?

Perhaps the first words from the child will disclose drug use or vague allegations of abuse, neglect, or emotional harm by the custodial parent. What if the parent who brings the child to treatment wants to be better positioned in a custody battle and is intending to call the therapist as a witness and to subpoena the child's records in order to prevail in the litigation, or has unduly influenced the child in order to prompt a child abuse report by the treating therapist?

Such occurrences often take place. If the therapist initially requires notice to or the consent of the other parent before undertaking treatment, such hidden parental agendas may be brought to light and becoming enmeshed in the parents' domestic litigation can perhaps be avoided.

## Authorizations to Release Information

When treating a child with parental consent, the general rule is that either parent can sign an authorization form to release confidential information about the child's treatment to a third party. A parent who has sole legal custody would ordinarily sign an authorization form on behalf of the minor. If there is joint legal custody, the general rule is that either parent can sign the authorization form, unless the court order has specified otherwise.

Some states recognize a minor's right to control release of confidential information. If state law permits the minor to consent to the treatment without knowledge or consent of the parent, the minor must sign the authorization form. Depending on the law of the state, that age can be as young as 12.

The ability of a minor to consent to treatment without parental consent can also be established by emancipation of the minor. Emancipation generally involves a legal proceeding. It can also result from parental consent or marriage.

## Complaints to the Licensing Board

Licensing boards receive a large number and significant percentage of complaints from people who are involved in custody or visitation disputes. A disgruntled spouse may disagree with a therapist's findings or opinions, or may blame the therapist for a judge's adverse order. The more sophisticated licensing boards, and those who investigate or make decisions regarding closing or pursuing a case, are usually aware that many of these complaints, especially those that allege that the therapist unlawfully treated the child without the consent of the complainant, are without merit.

Nevertheless, therapists who receive licensing board requests for answers to specific questions, or those who receive calls from a state investigator wanting to discuss a complaint, would generally be well advised to consult with a lawyer knowledgeable in state administrative proceedings.

It is always the therapist's choice whether or not to undertake treatment of children or adults involved in litigation. It is also the therapist's choice whether or not to participate in the litigation by writing letters, reports, or treatment summaries, and risk antagonizing one or both parents.

## Chapter 8
# Confidentiality When Working with Couples and Families

When treating a couple or family, the therapist may decide to see one or more of the participants individually for one or more sessions, then return to seeing the couple or family in future sessions. Are the individual sessions to be viewed as part of the couple or family therapy? Are the individuals told that such is the case? Are they led to believe that the individual sessions are completely confidential, even as it relates to others participating in the therapy and even if the therapist believes that it is information that should be shared with the unit being treated in order for the couple or family work to be effective? It is important to be clear with participants in therapy and to let them know how you will handle such issues.

AAMFT's Code of Ethics recognizes that the "client" in a therapeutic relationship may be more than one person. Thus, it is commonly understood that the client may be a couple or a family. The ethical standards also state that marriage and family therapists disclose to "clients" the **nature of confidentiality** and **possible limitations on the clients' right to confidentiality**. If there are limitations, the disclosure is to be made as early as feasible in the professional relationship. Thus, prior to the commencement of couple or family therapy, it would be wise for therapists to inform the participants about the nature and extent of confidentiality as it relates to the services being sought.

Generally, the laws of confidentiality are intended to prevent unauthorized disclosures to third parties. If the identified client is a couple, most MFTs understand that before they release information about the couple, or any one of them, to a third party, they must obtain the written authorization of the client — that is, both persons who are participating in the couples work. If the therapist needs to see one or both of the participants for a few sessions individually, and then intends to return to working with both, it is important for the therapist to let the parties know that the couple remains the identified client, and that these sessions are to be considered a part of the process of couple therapy. This will probably confirm the belief of the participants.

What if the individual being seen now wanted the therapist to release only his individual records to a third party? The therapist would likely take the view that the signature of both or all parties would be needed, since these sessions, although with only one of the participants, were considered by all to be a part of the couples or family work. The therapist typically is not likely to have told the individuals involved that the therapeutic relationship with the couple or family was temporarily being terminated, or that the therapist was now beginning a new and separate professional relationship with the individual. The therapist's allegiance is to the client — that is, the couple or family.

Thus, when the parties are told that the individual sessions are a necessary part of the work with the couple or family, and that the therapist's primary allegiance and duty is to the client — that is, the couple or family, what is the individual to think about the confidentiality of his/her communications with the therapist during those individual sessions? Isn't it reasonable for the client to expect that the communications will be confidential? What should the individual be told about the limitation to confidentiality? The "no secrets" policy (see below) is intended to answer those questions.

Not all communications from a client to a therapist are confidential. The law of confidentiality, from its very origins, was never intended to be absolute. If the client threatens imminent physical harm to self or others, most state laws require or allow disclosure without the written authorization of the client. Child and elder abuse reporting laws require certain disclosures to be made. If the client utters words to his therapist in the waiting room and in the presence of others, there is generally no right to confidentiality with respect to that communication.

What the therapist is really telling the client by using a "no secrets" policy is that, while confidentiality is generally going to be protected and respected, it may become necessary for the therapist, in the reasonable exercise of clinical judgment, and in order to treat the client properly, to disclose certain information learned in the individual session to the actual client — that is, to the couple or the family (though not to a third party). The therapist will ultimately decide whether or not any disclosure needs to be made, what specific disclosures may be necessary, when the disclosure should be made, and by whom the disclosure should be made — all for the appropriate treatment of the couple or family. Such a disclosure should not be seen as an inappropriate or unlawful breach of the duty of confidentiality, but rather, as a necessary part of therapy.

It is important, again, to point out that such disclosures are not going to be made, if they are made at all, to a third party, but rather, to the client or client (the couple or family). The disclosures, if any, will be made in the best interests of the client and for treatment purposes, and for no other purpose. With the signature of all of the participants acknowledging the policy, they have been informed of both the nature of confidentiality and the possible limitation upon confidentiality as it pertains to couple or family work. They have also given the therapist their written permission to make the disclosures that are described in the policy.

The written permission obtained in this instance is not permission sought immediately prior to a desired disclosure, but rather, permission gained prior to the commencement of therapy and, in essence, as a precondition to embarking upon a course of couple or family therapy.

# "No Secrets" Policy For Couple or Family Treatment

*NOTE: This sample "no secrets" policy is intended to help therapists anticipate certain problems that may occur when providing therapy to couples or families. If any of the statements made in this sample policy do not accurately reflect your views or your method of practice, you should not include them in any policy that you may choose to use. The title of the form could be something other than a "No Secrets Policy", perhaps "Limitation on Confidentiality when Providing Therapy to Couples or Families." This sample is provided solely for information and educational purposes and should not be considered to be legal advice.*

This statement of policy is intended to inform you, the participants in therapy, that when I agree to treat a couple or a family, I consider that couple or family (the treatment unit) to be the client. For instance, if there is a request for the treatment records of the couple or the family, I will seek the authorization of all members of the treatment unit before I release confidential information to third parties. Also, if my records are subpoenaed, I will assert the psychotherapist-patient privilege on behalf of the client (treatment unit).

During the course of my work with a couple or a family, I may see a smaller part of the treatment unit (e.g., an individual or two siblings) for one or more sessions. These sessions should be seen by you as a part of the work that I am doing with the family or the couple, unless otherwise indicated. If you are involved in one or more of such sessions with me, please understand that generally these sessions are confidential in the sense that I will not release any confidential information to a third party unless I am required by law to do so, or unless I have your written authorization. In fact, since those sessions can and should be considered a part of the treatment of the couple or family, I would also seek the authorization of the other individuals in the treatment unit before releasing confidential information to a third party.

However, I may need to share information learned in an individual session (or a session with only a portion of the treatment unit being present) with the entire treatment unit —— that is, the family or the couple, if I am effectively to serve the unit being treated. I will use my best judgment as to whether, when, and to what extent I will make disclosures to the treatment unit, and I will also, if appropriate, first give the individual or the smaller part of the treatment unit being seen the opportunity to make the disclosure. Thus, if you feel it necessary to talk about matters that you absolutely want to be shared with no one, you might want to consult with an individual therapist who can treat you individually.

This "no secrets" policy is intended to allow me to continue to treat the couple or family by preventing, to the extent possible, a conflict of interest to arise where an individual's interests may not be consistent with the interests of the unit being treated. For instance, information learned in the course of an individual session may be relevant or even essential to the proper treatment of the couple or the family. If I am not free to exercise my clinical judgment regarding the need to bring this information to the family or the couple during their therapy, I might be placed in a situation where I will have to terminate treatment of the couple or the family. This policy is intended to prevent the need for such a termination.

By signing below, you, as members of the couple/family or other unit receiving treatment, acknowledge that each of you has read this policy, that you understand it, that you have had an opportunity to discuss its contents with me as your therapist, and that you undertake couple/family therapy in agreement with this policy.

Date_____          Signature _____

Date_____          Signature _____

Date_____          Signature _____

*(Use additional date and signature lines as is necessary. If someone is signing in a representative capacity, such as a parent or a court-appointed guardian or conservator, such capacity should be stated and the person being represented should be specified.)*

## Chapter 9
# Confidentiality In A Court-Ordered Therapy Setting

*I'm treating a bioDad and two minor children who were ordered by the domestic relations judge to undergo therapy. I wrote a report for the Court recommending unsupervised visitation with bioMom. BioDad has filed a complaint with my licensing board.*

Subprinciple 3.14: To avoid a conflict of interests, marriage and family therapists who treat minors or adults involved in custody or visitation actions may not also perform forensic evaluations for custody, residence, or visitation of the minor. The marriage and family therapist who treats the minor may provide the court or mental health professional performing the evaluation with information about the minor from the marriage and family therapist's perspective as a treating marriage and family therapist, so long as the marriage and family therapist does not violate confidentiality.

An emerging issue in ethics and legal consultations involves confidentiality and conflict of interest for members who take on court-ordered therapy clients or clients who are otherwise involved in family court proceedings after those proceedings have begun.

A family court judge orders divorcing parties to family therapy. A family court judge orders reunification between a mother and children prior to entering a custody order. A single mom who is trying to stop the Department of Child Services from terminating her parental rights is ordered to get therapy.

Does a therapist/client relationship exist? Can parties who seek therapy as the result of a court order give informed consent? What is the limit on confidentiality protections for a client unit/participant where the object of the therapy is a report to the court or to Child Services? What protection does a therapist who provides therapy in such a situation have from a malpractice claim or complaint to the State licensing board by the participant who loses more as a result of the Judge's order based on the therapist's report?

A therapist in Tennessee has had her license placed on probation for one year because she "provided psychotherapy" to two minor children, their parents and their stepmother. She recommended to the Court that the father's visitation rights be terminated. The father filed a complaint with the Tennessee Board. The therapist was found to have acted in a dual capacity as a clinician and forensic evaluator.

It is critical when undertaking court-ordered therapy that everyone understand what the object of the therapy is, whether and to whom the therapist is required to report about the therapy, and what the limits of confidentiality are when the clients participate because they are required to. A special or limited-purpose informed consent document may be appropriate in these circumstances.

# Chapter 10
# Testifying Or Writing A Letter For A Client Or Client's Lawyer

*I've been treating a bioMom who lost custody of her children two years ago. She wants me to write a letter on her behalf to the guardian ad litem in the custody proceeding.*

Subprinciple 1.3: Marriage and family therapists are aware of their influential positions with respect to clients, and they avoid exploiting the trust and dependency of such persons. Therapists, therefore, make every effort to avoid conditions and multiple relationships with clients that could impair professional judgment or increase the risk of exploitation. Such relationships include, but are not limited to, business or close personal relationships with a client or the client's immediate family. When the risk of impairment or exploitation exists due to conditions or multiple roles, therapists take appropriate precautions.

Subprinciple 3.14: To avoid a conflict of interests, marriage and family therapists who treat minors or adults involved in custody or visitation actions may not also perform forensic evaluations for custody, residence, or visitation of the minor. . . . .

The minute the therapist agrees to write a letter, or testify, or talk to the lawyer, the therapist ceases to be a therapist and becomes an advocate.

The situation is even more complicated if the therapist has seen the children and/or the custodial father as part of the mother's treatment or prior to it. The father will be the first to file a licensing board complaint or malpractice suit alleging bias and breach of confidentiality.

Whether or not writing a letter to the GAL is a "forensic evaluation" so that it would be a conflict of interest under 3.14 is always a question of fact. A letter that offers an opinion on whether or not custody should be modified is clearly a forensic evaluation and the responsibility of an expert. A treating therapist cannot be an expert.

As difficult as it may be, the

therapist must not be a helper in this situation. In addition to the ethical considerations, the reality is that if the decision in the custody proceeding goes against the bioMom/client, it's possible that the therapeutic relationship will be adversely affected.

## Chapter 11
# Termination of Treatment – Legal and Ethical Considerations

There are a variety of considerations and potential problems connected with termination of treatment. If the process of termination is not properly carried out, the attempt to end therapy can constitute an abandonment of the client, which may result in a complaint to the licensing board or a civil action for damages. Additionally, a failure to pay attention to the issue of termination may result in a therapist being held liable for harm to the client, even though the therapist was under the impression that the therapist-client relationship had ended.

Generally, clients have the right to terminate treatment at any time and for any reason. Therapists commonly terminate treatment a) when the course of treatment has come to a natural end because of the improvement of the client, b) when the client is no longer able to pay for treatment pursuant to the original agreement, c) when the therapist has determined that the client's problem is beyond the therapist's scope of competence, d) when the therapist determines that the client is not benefiting from the treatment, e) when the therapist is unable or unwilling, for appropriate reasons, to continue to provide care, or f) when the treating therapist leaves his or her employment, either voluntarily or involuntarily.

## Unwilling or Unable to Continue to Provide Care

There are many situations that may justify or require termination by the therapist under this category. Perhaps the client is not attending sessions regularly or canceling sessions to such a degree that the therapist believes adequate treatment is compromised, and the client's problem cannot be resolved, or may even be worsened, by such pattern of attendance. Perhaps a client is not willing to take the therapist's referrals to a physician for a physical examination or evaluation for medication, or to others for recommended diagnosis or treatment. Perhaps a conflict arises that, in the opinion of the therapist, requires a termination.

Additionally, therapists may retire, move, or be forced to suspend, close or limit their practices due to illness or other reasons. Clients should be informed of the impending termination well in advance of a planned retirement, and with as much prior notice as circumstances permit or clinical considerations dictate in other cases. Wherever possible, the termination should be discussed with the client and provisions should be made for the continued care of the client.

# Discharge from Employment

When a therapist leaves an employed position, either voluntarily or involuntarily, what communications should occur with the client? Therapists who are discharged with little prior notice express concerns about the client, and often want to contact the client in an effort to have the client follow them to their new location, or to explain why the therapist will not be present at the next session. This is usually not a good idea. The therapist is generally best served by promptly contacting the employer by telephone (later confirmed in writing) to express concerns about the client because of the sudden termination.

The therapist can request that the employer inform the client of the client's options – that is, to remain at the agency and see another therapist, to leave the agency and be referred elsewhere or to continue to see the departing therapist at the therapist's new location, unless the terms of the therapist's employment prohibit it. The therapist should remind the employer of the importance of continuity of care and the duty to act in the client's best interests. The therapist can also let the employer know, if appropriate, that the employer bears responsibility for any client harm due to the sudden and inappropriate termination of the therapist and the failure to inform fully the client of his or her options.

If the termination takes place over a period of time, as when the therapist gives notice that she is leaving, the therapist can inform the client of the options. Often, the employer will protest and will not want the client to follow the departing therapist, or even be informed of the options available. Again, all parties have a duty to act in the client's best interests. Sometimes, the employer tries to enforce a written agreement where the therapist has either promised not to take take employer clients to the new location, or where the therapist has agreed to pay money to the employer for doing so..

# Disclosure Statements and Termination

Many therapists use some form of disclosure statement, either because it is legally required or because the therapist finds it useful in establishing the ground rules for the commencement of a professional relationship. Typically included in these statements are such matters as the therapists' treatment philosophy or approach to therapy, their credentials, their hours of availability, what to do in cases of an emergency, the fee to be charged for services and information about confidentiality and the exceptions thereto. The issue of termination can also be addressed in the disclosure statement, which may prove helpful to the therapist at the time of termination.

The disclosure statement can explain that the client has the right to terminate at any time and for any reason. The therapist may want to state a preference that if the client desires to terminate the relationship, the client should discuss termination with the therapist in advance so that there can be proper closure, including referrals where appropriate, and so that any misunderstandings may be resolved. While the client may ultimately choose to ignore this stated preference, it is quite reasonable and professional at the inception of therapy.

It may also prove useful to inform the client, in the statement, that if the client is unable to continue to pay the agreed upon fee, the client should speak with the therapist promptly so that the therapist can decide whether or not treatment will continue (perhaps the therapist will lower the fee or work pro bono for a period of time), or whether treatment will be terminated and a referral made.

Perhaps most helpful, especially in difficult cases, is for the disclosure statement to inform the client that the therapist is ethically bound to terminate therapy when it is reasonably clear that the client is not benefiting from the therapy. Many therapists have experienced the difficult client who may not be willing to let go of the relationship. Letting the client know, early in the process, of one's ethical duties in this regard may ease the termination process with such clients.

## Process of Termination

Therapists who get in trouble are those who, with little or no prior discussion with the client, terminate treatment, perhaps by writing a letter, speaking on the telephone or leaving a message. Ethical practice usually demands more. Terminations initiated by the therapist should generally be the result of a process where the client is given time to meet with the therapist to discuss the reasons for the termination, and where transition to other care, if appropriate or necessary, is discussed. In general, the longer the therapeutic relationship has been in effect, the longer the period of time needed for the termination process.

Although sessions held for the purpose of discussing termination issues are a part of the therapy process and are properly billed for, therapists may want to consider waiving some or all of the fee in order to lessen the burden on the client. With respect to the issue of transition to other care, therapists must not only be prepared to make thoughtful referrals, but must also think about making a reasonable effort to follow through with the client to determine whether or not the client is receiving the recommended care.

In some cases, a client may not show up for one or more sessions and may not respond to inquiries by the therapist. Failure to clarify the client's status could result in problems for the therapist, since the client may later claim that there was never a termination, just a lull in the treatment. When the client later calls in crisis, it may be difficult for the therapist to maintain that there had been a termination and that he or she is not accepting "new" clients. If the therapist fails to treat the client when he or she re-presents, this could lead to a charge of abandonment — at the time that the client claims to be most in need.

Termination by the therapist is most difficult with clients who are in serious emotional distress, including those who are suicidal or those who feign suicide. The client will often be reluctant to end the relationship even though a termination may, in the opinion of the therapist, be in the best interests of the client. In such situations (and others), it is useful to obtain one or more clinical consultations. A termination in these circumstances may require the therapist to warn others of the client's suicidal threats. State law usually either allows or compels disclosure when the client is in such mental or emotional condition as to be a danger to self and when disclosure is necessary to avert such danger.

## Who Is the Client?

Therapists often have trouble identifying the client. Perhaps the original identified client was a couple, but it later turned into individual therapy when one of the participants dropped out of therapy. Perhaps the therapist was working with an individual, but the therapy later turned into couple or family therapy.

While it is sometimes difficult to pigeonhole treatment into one category or another, therapists should pay attention to the question of client identity so that they can be clear — both to the participants directly and in the records – when the therapist-client relationship changes. It may be necessary or advisable to let one or more of the participants know that there has been a termination of a prior relationship, and that, for the future, a different relationship exists.

## Dual Relationships and Termination

It is usually my advice that dual or multiple relationships are to be avoided both during the therapist-client relationship and following a termination. However, some states' laws (and AAMFT's Code of Ethics) do not prohibit even a sexual relationship between a therapist and a former client following the two-year period of time after termination of the therapeutic relationship. A therapist who is going to engage in any kind of post-therapy relationship with a former client must be certain that the termination process was "clean" and uncontaminated.

A termination initiated for the purpose of engaging in a post-therapy relationship, arguable, is not a proper termination and the two-year rule (if sex is involved) is inapplicable. If, however, the termination occurred because the course of treatment ended for appropriate clinical reasons, and a relationship later develops without any contemplation of such relationship while therapy was occurring, a different situation exists. With respect to nonsexual relationships with former clients, such as friendship or business relationships, therapists must be careful that enough time has passed from the date of termination such that the risks of exploitation and impairment of judgment have been eliminated.

A major problem with any kind of post-therapy relationship is that the therapist is always at risk for a charge that the therapist improperly foreclosed the client's right to future care in order to satisfy the therapist's current needs (exploitation).

## Termination Letters

The termination process should be well documented in the treatment records, regardless of who initiates the termination. When the process goes smoothly, there may be no need to confirm the termination by letter. When the termination process is more volatile, it is more likely that the therapist may want to send a letter to confirm the termination and the reasons for it, including who initiated the termination. In more ambiguous situations, where, for example, a client simply doesn't show up for appointments, the therapist may want first to reach out to the client in an effort to clarify the client's intentions. This can usually be done by telephone and confirmed thereafter in writing.

Before writing to a client, the therapist must have permission from the client to send letters to the client at a particular address. The letter must be carefully drafted and must be an accurate reflection of what has occurred. It should be consistent with the records and, to the extent possible, not be inflammatory. If the client later decides to take action against the therapist, the therapist must be able to defend the appropriateness of each statement in the letter. Before sending such a letter, therapists would be wise to consult with a respected colleague or with legal counsel.

While termination letters may be appropriate, some form of personal communication with documentation of the conversation in the records may be less taxing. Following the personal communication (often by telephone), it is usually easier to write a letter confirming the essence of the conversation, including the reasons for the termination. Sometimes a letter will simply confirm the fact that, despite several attempts by the therapist, the client fails to respond or refuses to discuss the issue.

If the termination involves a referral of the client to a different therapist, consider confirming the referral(s) in writing, and making a statement of a specific window of availability to permit the client to make the transfer. "Please feel free to contact me at any time for the next two weeks," may help avoid a complaint for abandonment.

## Chapter 12
# Client Suicide

When the unthinkable happens, self-care is important. Consulting with a colleague and time to reflect before being drawn into the inevitable aftermath of a client suicide are essential.

You are not expected to predict suicide. You are not expected to prevent suicide. Your duty extends to protecting a client.

Suppose you receive a call from a police officer reporting the death of your client and wanting to talk with you as part of an investigation. Or a family member calls you to report that your client committed suicide last night and the family needs a copy of the file for the inquest.

Before you take any steps, even if you suspect that the client may not have been a suicide, take a moment to locate the client file and call your malpractice carrier. YOU ARE NOT ADMITTING LIABILITY OR SUBJECTING YOURSELF TO ADVERSE ACTION. The insurance company will be able to advise you of appropriate next steps that will help you and the insurance company if there should ever be a claim made against you in the future.

Consulting with your professional liability carrier will give you access to information that will help you respond appropriately. For example, if there is no exception to the rules

governing confidentiality, you may need to invoke the privilege until it is waived by an appropriate individual.

Finally, accurate documentation and comprehensive risk assessment helps reduce liability. Although errors of judgment (failure accurately to assess suicide potential) are inevitable, errors of omission (failure adequately to assess suicide potential) are preventable.

*Section C*

# The Therapist
# and the Court

# Chapter 1
# **The Subpoena**

A subpoena taped to your office door, handed to you by a process server or delivered in the mail, is annoying at best and alarming at worst. It is the first step in a pageant in which you have no choice but to participate. It can be helpful to prepare ahead of time and know what steps to take and when to take them.

Questions about the subpoena top the list of calls and e-mails to AAMFT's Legal Consultation service. Some MFTs are attempting to avoid being subpoenaed into court by including provisions in an informed consent document advising the client that the therapist will not participate in litigation. While this type of notice to a client may have some limiting effect, whether or not it is enforceable has yet to be tested. Further, it is often the opposing side that issues the subpoena.

An attorney issues a subpoena so that the client's case can be proved by introducing documents or testimony into evidence. A subpoena is a process of the courts, not of the parties. Although a subpoena may be issued by an attorney, it is a mandate of the court, issued for the court.

A subpoena is an order of a sort. The Latin root translates as "under penalty." The recipient of a subpoena is commanded to appear "under penalty" of contempt. Failure to show up and testify, either at deposition or at trial, and/or to produce documents (subpoena duces tecum—"bring with you") can result in an order of contempt against the therapist, meaning fines and payment of attorneys' fees.

Do not let the word "order" in a subpoena confuse you, or the lawyer issuing the subpoena intimidate you. A subpoena is not the type of court order that permits a client's confidentiality to be breached. Therapists are trained to preserve confidentiality.

A therapist's first response to a subpoena should be to resist, thereby protecting the client. But the resistance needs to be well thought out and properly executed in order to avoid a finding of contempt.If you receive a subpoena, read it. If you overcome your aversion to fine print and legalese, the subpoena will tell you the names of the parties, the date, time and place you will need to appear, the name of the lawyer who issued the subpoena, and the location and type of court in which the lawsuit is taking place.

When you have gleaned the basic information from the subpoena and identified which of your clients is involved, determine whether the attorney issuing the subpoena is the attorney for your client or the attorney for the party opposing your client. The identity of the subpoena issuer is significant in regard to protecting your client's confidentiality, and because of privilege that you may be able to invoke on your client's behalf. This is important not only for your client, but also for you, since you could be liable to your client for breaching confidentiality and subject to discipline by your licensing board for unethical or unprofessional conduct.

If the attorney issuing the subpoena represents your client, you could conclude that the client has waived the "psychotherapist-client" privilege and that you are not breaching your duty to the client by turning over the requested documents or testifying at a deposition or at trial. However, AAMFT's Code of Ethics and most state laws governing confidentiality require that a waiver be in writing. It is in your best interest to "invoke the privilege" if the subpoena is not accompanied by a signed waiver.

If, however, the attorney issuing the subpoena represents the opposing party, the subpoena must have a release signed by your client attached to it. If there is no signed release, you need to protect your client's confidentiality and invoke the "psychotherapist-client" privilege on your client's behalf.

Fax or mail the issuing attorney a letter advising that you have received the subpoena but that it lacks a release from the client authorizing you to disclose the confidential information requested. Without that release, you can neither confirm nor deny whether a therapist/client relationship exists.

Some attorneys will acknowledge the privilege and volunteer to secure the appropriate releases. Others will threaten you with contempt for ignoring a court order. That the subpoena is a court order is true, so far as it goes. But in breaching a client's confidentiality, a subpoena does not offer the therapist sufficient protection. Do not be intimidated by threats or rants. All states recognize a mental health professional/client privilege in one way or another.

The absence of a release or waiver of privilege by the client is more significant for the therapist who has been treating a couple or family. The client unit (couple, family or group) holds the privilege and all participants must waive the privilege before the therapist can lawfully and ethically produce documents or give testimony about any participant in the couple, family or group. Without that waiver, law and ethics require an order, signed by a judge, directing the therapist by name to produce testimony or documents.

Such an order protects the therapist in two areas. First, all licensing statutes require professional conduct and ethical practice on the part of license holders.

Those same licensing statutes identify breach of client confidentiality as an instance of unprofessional conduct or unethical practice. Therefore, a therapist who complies with a subpoena without releases or waivers from all clients puts the license at risk for denial, revocation or suspension.

Second, a therapist who breaches a client's confidentiality without the court ordering the disclosure is at risk for an allegation of malpractice. The therapist owes a duty of confidentiality to the client. The therapist provided testimony or produced documents without a waiver from the client, breaching that duty.

The therapist is liable for damage resulting from that breach of duty.

If the issuing attorney threatens contempt or other proceedings, you can assure the attorney that you have no intention of not appearing in response to the subpoena. You are just trying to save time and the expense to you of filing a motion to quash the subpoena based on the existence of the privilege and the absence of a release from your client.

Also keep in mind that you are within your rights to refuse to speak to the attorney and to request that all communication be in writing.

## Subpoena Checklist:

- Where are you required to appear?

- Are you required to bring documents with you?

- When are you required to appear?
  If you are required to appear for a deposition with less than one week's notice, and that presents a problem for you in terms of management of your office and your clients, call the attorney issuing the subpoena and request a change in date.

- Does the subpoena contain a check for witness fees and expenses?
  You may call the attorney issuing the subpoena and find out how long the deposition or hearing is expected to continue. Request a witness fee in the amount of that number of hours times your hourly fee. This does not guarantee you'll receive payment, and you cannot condition your showing up on being paid.

- Does the subpoena contain a release signed by your client authorizing you to testify and/or produce documents?
  If the subpoena does not have a release, notify the attorney issuing the subpoena that you are invoking the client's privilege (see above). You can call the client, but it is not your responsibility to secure the releases. The issuing attorney is seeking privileged information and, in order to get it, the attorney must provide proof that the privilege has been waived.

- The issuing attorney may suggest that a subpoena is a court order and that failure to comply is contempt of court. Don't panic. Remind the issuing attorney that you are not threatening not to appear, but you are advising that you intend to preserve confidentiality until you are assured that it has been waived, either by the client or by a court order.

- Your license to practice can be denied, suspended or revoked for unprofessional conduct or a breach of the Code of Ethics. Breach of confidentiality is both an instance of unprofessional conduct and a breach of ethics. If you comply with the subpoena without a release or a court order, your license to practice is at risk. Therefore, and as a courtesy, you are informing the issuing attorney that you require protection in the form of either a release by the client or a court order signed by a judge who has reviewed your claim of privilege.

- Be prepared to contact your malpractice carrier for assistance in filing a motion to quash the subpoena or for a protective order. Your professional liability coverage may provide payment for legal fees and expenses related to subpoenas.

In the event you have additional questions, please take advantage of the AAMFT's Legal Consultation service. Legal consultation services are provided to AAMFT Clinical Members in legal matters relating to their professional practice of marriage and family therapy. The service includes telephone consultation during office hours (Eastern time). Please call (703) 253-0471 to speak to a lawyer or to schedule an appointment.

## Chapter 2
# Understanding Privilege

Many mental health practitioners are unclear about the difference between confidentiality and privilege. The distinction is important, and understanding the difference between the two concepts is essential to an understanding of how to respond to a subpoena

Simply put, confidentiality is a general restriction (by law and by ethical standards) on the volunteering of information pertaining to your client, while privilege involves the right to withhold testimony or records in a legal proceeding. It is important for mental health practitioners to know whether or not they are covered by a psychotherapist-patient privilege (the privilege may be called something else), and whether or not the privilege applies in both civil and criminal cases. This article assumes that the reader is fully covered by the privilege.

The general rule is that no person has a right to refuse to testify in a legal proceeding if properly subpoenaed. Likewise, the general rule is that documents/records may be obtained in a legal proceeding if a lawful subpoena is issued, and no person can refuse to produce such evidence.

There are exceptions to these general rules based on specific well-recognized and confidential relationships. The primary privileges recognized by most state laws are the attorney-client, physician-patient, clergy-penitent, psychotherapist-client, and husband-wife privileges. The patient, client, penitent or spouse can generally prevent the therapist, attorney, spouse or clergyperson from disclosing information or records by claiming, asserting, or invoking the privilege.

Legislatures have decided that there is a greater societal benefit in excluding this kind of evidence in legal proceedings than there is in allowing the court to have the benefit of

the evidence, even though the information may be relevant to the issues involved. The greater public benefit in excluding the testimony is that people will be encouraged to communicate fully and openly with their therapists (and others covered by a privilege) so that they can get the help that they need without the fear that their confidential communications or records will later be revealed in a legal proceeding.

Your treatment of your client is a confidential matter. Without your client's authorization to disclose that treatment, since you are required by your licensing law to protect client confidentiality, you must invoke the therapist/client privilege.

That privilege belongs to the client. If the client waives it, you must disclose whatever information the client authorizes you to disclose. But with the signed waiver in your file, the client cannot later complain that you breached your duty of maintaining client confidentiality.

## When The Subpoena Arrives

The subpoena will probably be from the attorney for the adverse party in a civil proceeding. If your client's attorney wanted your records, all he/she would need to do is make a request for them and provide you with the client's authorization. Even if it is the client's attorney asking for records, that request should always be in writing.

It is not uncommon for the opposing party's attorney to hire someone to serve you with a subpoena for records. If that subpoena does not have a release or authorization signed by your client attached, you would immediately notify the issuing attorney that you are asserting the psychotherapist-patient privilege, and refuse to release the records.

After you have accepted the subpoena and claimed the privilege, it is the responsibility of the issuing attorney to obtain a release from the client or an order from the court waiving the privilege and permitting you to produce the records without risking a breach of client confidentiality.

Some lawyers recommend that you contact your client to let her/him know that you received a subpoena for her/his records. If the client is still in treatment, this involves you in the client's life outside of therapy. It is often the case that your client doesn't know the lawyers' legal strategy, and the subpoena will be a surprise. The client may or may not have a lawyer. It's usually simpler to give notice to the issuing attorney that you are invoking the privilege with a copy of that notice to your client or the client's attorney.

## Attorney Contact

If, with your client's permission, you contact her/his attorney, the attorney cannot ethically give you advice about handling the subpoena. Since you have already invoked the privilege on behalf of the client, you have discharged your obligation.

The attorney who issued the subpoena may call you to argue whether or not a waiver of privilege is required. You do not need to engage with any attorney over the telephone. Ask that the attorney send you a letter so that you can review it and so that your record will be complete. If the attorney threatens to ask the court to hold you in contempt for noncompliance, you can let him/her know that you have the documentation to show that the privilege has not been waived, and that you'll be happy to let the judge know that you were following the rules by claiming the client's privilege.

## Protective Orders

Many clients do not realize that if they are suing for mental or emotional distress, their mental state is an issue in the lawsuit, and the privilege has probably been waived giving the opposition access to all of their records and to the therapist's testimony.

However, as the therapist invoking the client's privilege, you need not rely on an attorney involved in the litigation telling you that this is the case.

Some states have a procedure whereby the attorney seeking the records gives notice to the client's attorney that a subpoena will be served on the therapist, and, unless the client's attorney objects, any privilege will be considered waived. This type of proceeding can be confusing to a therapist who receives a copy of a subpoena along with a notice that the subpoena will be served in 30 days.

If the client does not object, the therapist receives the actual, signed subpoena, but there is still no release attached. Since most licensing statutes require that a client's waiver of confidentiality be in writing, the therapist is still at some risk for releasing information, even though the client did not object. This further embroils the therapist in the client's legal issues.

In this situation, the therapist should consider asking the court for a protective order, especially if the records are those of a client unit in treatment (e.g., a couple or a family) and only one member of that unit is involved in litigation. A protective order is a court order of the type that protects the therapist who discloses confidential information without a written waiver from the client.

In this situation, your malpractice carrier may provide payment for legal representation for you to avoid a future claim that you breached the client's confidentiality.

## Determining Privilege

Perhaps you are treating a person under the age of eighteen. In some states, the holder of the privilege is the minor (since the minor is the client), even where the minor is a very young child. If records were subpoenaed in one of those states, the therapist would assert the privilege on behalf of the child and not release the records unless ordered by the court or unless authorized by the child's attorney or some other person appointed by the court to represent the interests of the child in the legal proceeding. While parents are the natural guardians of their children and generally exercise legal control of them, when it comes to privilege, the parents may not hold the privilege.

It is important to know who the client is because you may need to assert privilege on his/her/their behalf. Thus, a couple or an entire family might well be the holder of the privilege, and a waiver may not be fully effective unless all parties in the unit waive the privilege. The general rule is that if persons are in therapy to further the interests of a particular client (or each other) in the consultation or the treatment, the privilege is not waived by the presence of those other persons. This general rule should protect the privilege in cases involving group therapy, couples therapy, or family therapy. With respect to a deceased client, the privilege generally survives the death of the client and the personal representative of the deceased would usually be a holder of the privilege.

Each case is different and state laws vary. You should obtain a legal consultation whenever you are uncertain about how to proceed. If you make a mistake in this area of practice, it is usually better if you make a mistake by withholding production of the records than if you make a mistake by releasing the records. Remember, your first instinct when served with a subpoena for records should be to resist. If you are covered by the psychotherapist-patient privilege, your duty is to assert the privilege and protect the client's privacy until properly instructed otherwise by your client or the court.

## Chapter 3
# The Treating Therapist As Witness

When your client or the client's lawyer asks you to participate in a case, the lawyer is almost always looking for an expert opinion. To a lawyer or court, "expert" means someone who is qualified to give opinions at trial. It doesn't mean superstar or genius, but merely a person whose background and experience impresses a court enough to allow an opinion about something. Fact or "lay" witnesses testify about what they have seen, heard, felt.

You may feel compelled to testify for your own current or past client, and the lawyer may try to ease you into it by starting out with simple questions about the course of your treatment, and then asking for an opinion. Don't do it. There is a substantial conflict of interest between treating and expert roles.

Attorneys often refer their clients for treatment, assuming the therapist will testify if needed. Beware of lawyers (and clients) who would place you in an unethical position. Once a person is your client, you must act in the client's interest. You cannot be an expert and objective, even if you believe you can. When a lawyer sends a client for treatment, make it clear to the attorney and the client that you will not be available for expert testimony. Both you and the client should be aware that if the referral has anything to do with litigation, the treatment will also be compromised to some degree by the possibility that the other side could subpoena the records.

The function of therapist and advocate is clearly a dual relationship. A treatment

relationship clearly creates a professional and ethical obligation to act in the best interests of the client.

The purpose and goals of the treating therapist are different from those of the expert witness. The clinician has fiduciary and ethical obligations to the client which demand that the client's interests be placed first.

## Chapter 4
# Clients Involved In Custody Disputes

There are two sources for information about the right of a parent to place a minor child in therapy and about the right of the "other" parent to the client child's mental health records.

One source is the custody order. If the parent who is placing the child in therapy tells you that the parents are divorced, ask for a copy of the custody order. This document will tell you which parent has custody of the client child and whether that custody is joint or sole, physical or legal.

Legal custody of a child means having the right and the obligation to make decisions about a child's upbringing. A parent with legal custody can make decisions about schooling, religion, and medical care, for example. In many states, courts regularly award joint legal custody, which means that the decision-making is shared by both parents.

Physical custody means that a parent has the right to have a child live with him or her. Some states will award joint physical custody to both parents when the child spends significant amounts of time with both parents. Where the child lives primarily with one parent and has visitation with the other, generally the parent with whom the child primarily lives will have sole physical custody, with visitation to the other parent.

The fact that legal custody is joint does not mean that one parent can stop the other from placing the child in therapy. Nor does it mean that the therapist must seek permission or authorization from the other parent to treat the child. It does mean that the other parent may be entitled to access to information about the child and the treatment.

If you do a fair amount of work with children of divorced parents, it may be appropriate to make your rules about access to the child's mental health record part of your informed consent document. Some states, and HIPAA's Privacy Rule, require that requests for protected health information in a client file be made in writing. You may also be entitled to deny a request for records if you believe that disclosure would be harmful to the child.

Don't forget to be clear about the identity of the client. If a custodial parent

seeks "family" therapy with the child, the client is the family and the Code of Ethics requires a written waiver from each individual in the client unit in order to disclose information outside the treatment context.

## Chapter 5
# Psychotherapy Notes

Under HIPAA's Privacy Rule, a client has certain rights with respect to the mental health record. State law may also give a client rights to records, but so far, the Privacy Rule and State records laws have not been found to be in conflict. Even if you are not a "covered provider," and required by HIPAA to provide a Notice of Privacy Practices, you might want to consider making the specifics of a request for records part of your informed consent document.

Under HIPAA's Privacy Rule, a client is entitled to inspect and copy the protected health information in the client's mental health record. The request must be in writing. Don't forget that if the client has more than one participant, under AAMFT's *Code of Ethics*, the participants who are not requesting the records must sign an authorization to disclose the information. It is the responsibility of the client making the request to provide the appropriate releases. You do not need to help the client make the request by telling him or her what to do.

The section of HIPAA's Privacy Rule that excludes psychotherapy notes can be found at 45 *Code of Federal Regulations* Section 164.524. It says that an individual is entitled to a copy of protected health information (essentially anything with a name or identifying number on it) **except** psychotherapy notes.

Psychotherapy notes are very specifically defined, but can be shorthanded to any recording by you, the therapist, of the content of a therapy session. If you scribble during session, if you make marks on a genogram or draw one, if you take five minutes after the client leaves to write down what was said, those are psychotherapy notes and the client (or the client's lawyer or somebody suing the client) has no right to a copy of them.

Psychotherapy notes record the content of a session. If you use those notes to prepare another document such as a treatment summary or referral, the document based on the notes is not protected. Psychotherapy notes must be separated from the rest of the record to be classified and protected as psycho-therapy notes.

Some states have laws that are specific

to records, to mental health records, and to the obligation of a mental health professional to provide records. You should be familiar with those records requirements if they exist in your state, especially if they speak to time limits for response or other specifics.

When you respond to a client's request for records, your cover letter should use the phrase "protected health information in your mental health record to which you have a right of access under HIPAA's Privacy Rule." This establishes that you are relying on and complying with the Privacy Rule.